A STRATEGIC PLAN
# ROSS MUELLER

CURRENCY PRESS

GTC
RHO
IEM
FAP
FTA
IRN
NEY

CURRENT THEATRE SERIES

First published in 2017
by Currency Press Pty Ltd,
PO Box 2287, Strawberry Hills, NSW, 2012, Australia
enquiries@currency.com.au
www.currency.com.au
in association with Griffin Theatre Company

Cataloguing-in-publication data for this title is available from the National
Library of Australia website: www.nla.gov.au

Typeset by Dean Nottle for Currency Press.
Cover image shows Justin Smith.
Cover photograph by Brett Boardman.
Cover design by RE:

Currency Press acknowledges the Traditional Owners of the Country on which
we live and work. We pay our respects to all Aboriginal and Torres Strait
Islander Elders, past and present.

# Contents

*This play is dedicated to Georgina Capper.*
*For her strength and her love, her sense of humour.*

*A Strategic Plan* was first produced by Griffin Theatre Company at SBW Stables Theatre, Sydney, on 27 January 2017, with the following cast:

| | |
|---|---|
| LINDA / LEANNE | Briallen Clarke |
| SIMON / PERKINS | Matt Day |
| ANDREW | Justin Smith |
| JILL | Emele Ugavule |

Director, Chris Mead
Designer, Sophie Fletcher
Lighting Designer, Verity Hampson
Sound Designer and Composer, Steve Francis
Design Assistant, Tyler Hawkins
Stage Manager, Grace Nye-Butler

## CHARACTERS

ANDREW, Director of Music Program
LEANNE, lawyer with a no-win no-fee law firm
LINDA, HR rep on Board of Management
SIMON, Chair of the Board of Management
JILL, Membership & Marketing employee
PERKINS, independent barrister

The casting should reflect the diversity of Australia.

Staccato, a not-for-profit organisation, promotes music and music opportunities for young people. It relies on government funding for survival.

A slash [/] indicates overlapping dialogue. If at the start of a line of dialogue, it indicates that the following line is to be spoken simultaneously.

This play went to press before the end of rehearsals and may differ from the play as performed.

*The Jam: 'Going Underground'.*

*SCENE ONE: CORE BUSINESS*

*Lights up on* ANDREW *and* JILL.

ANDREW *is in an airlock. Noise-cancelling headphones. Stainless steel water bottle. Listening to The Shanghai Susans. Plastic bags of folders at his feet. A grey-walled corridor only big enough for three humans and a table. Fluoro light above.*

JILL *is in her studio. She is setting up a couple of microphones. One for a vocal and one for acoustic guitar. Fluoro light.*

SIMON *is also onstage, either illuminated or in darkness.*

ANDREW *looks at the dead light. He claps his hands. Nothing. He tries again. Nothing. Silence.* LEANNE *arrives. Watches him. He moves his arms wildly in the air. Nothing. He jumps up and down and waves and claps.*

JILL *puts on headphones and tests the microphones with claps and clicks and ...*

JILL: One. Chew. One. Chew. One. Chooo. One ... Chew. Hello, hello. Hello, hello. / One two three four.

LEANNE: Are you okay?

SIMON: It is a fucking deathtrap.

JILL: Here we go. / Here we go. New man. Noi-man, N. E. U. Man. I got a D.I. for guitar and a second-hand Neu-mann T.L.M. one oh chew. One oh chew. Thank you, Georgie. Ho. Ho!

SIMON: And I happen to think that young people deserve a little bit better than derelict, dangerous, ex-government buildings, don't you? Oh no, that's right. You want to exterminate all the emerging artists in the world, don't you? Look at these walls—!

JILL: Hah! Ready for you—

LEANNE: Andrew?

ANDREW *takes off his headphones.*

ANDREW: Where have you been?

*Beat.*

LEANNE: Monday morning. Parking is a homicide.

ANDREW: It's polite to call if you're running late.

*The airlock scene continues as* LEANNE *sets up her workstation.*

LEANNE: Ando. I don't want to get off on the wrong foot but I am not late. / I am actually the best in the office when it comes time management and scheduling—I did my time in chambers with Gibson and Duncan and anybody who has survived articles with those two-time management Nazis knows how to read a clock on the wall. Gibson is the worst.

ANDREW: It is not 'Andy' or 'Ando' or 'The Drew-ster'. It's simple 'Andrew'. I'm renting and I've got a house inspection this morning, so I had to surgically clean my bathroom before I came here because my landlord is a neo-Nazi and she has pictures of every crack. Any tiny defect—

LEANNE: So far beyond anal, he is intestinal.

ANDREW: I left twenty minutes earlier than I needed just to make sure I would get here on time.

LEANNE: So did I, and look at me. / Here I am. On time. Ready to help you win.

ANDREW: Here I am. On time. They told me nine-thirty.

ANDREW'*s phone rings.*

LEANNE: For a ten a.m. start and—

ANDREW: [*answering*] Hello …?

LEANNE: He's answering his telephone. Good times.

ANDREW: Not even close. I have road cases for everything and … I know what … I am not going to negotiate. Five grand is rock bottom, or forget it.

*He hangs up.*

Fucken Gumtree.

LEANNE: You a local?

ANDREW: Moved here for the job.

LEANNE: Do you love it?

ANDREW: Cretins, bogans and Pizza Huts.

LEANNE: Awesome. So … What were you …? You know …? Got the whole … Peter Garrett thing—going—on … That was weird.

ANDREW: I thought it might respond.

*Beat.*

To human interaction.

*Beat.*

Government buildings. They come on when you move.

*Beat.*

But it didn't.

*Beat.*

So. We're in the dark.

LEANNE *hits the light switch. Fluoro buzzes into life.*

Oh. You have powers.

LEANNE: What have you got down there? Your whole life in plastic bags by the looks of it. Don't worry. I have copies of all the pertinent documents—

ANDREW: Have you read them?

LEANNE: That's my job. Now. The docket is always enormous on a Monday. A town this size—but the current state government believes—yes—so go and grab a coffee.

*Throughout the following,* LEANNE *gets a message and writes a response.*

ANDREW: There is a woman out there in / the foyer and … she has a black eye.

LEANNE: Yes. Yes … I know. There's a good place at the station.

ANDREW: Sorry. Am I interrupting you?

LEANNE: And send. What is that noise?

ANDREW: Shanghai Susans.

LEANNE: They're on Triple J.

ANDREW: You like 'em?

LEANNE: I don't know, they're fine.

ANDREW: Great bass. Like Kim Deal crossed with Carol Kaye.

LEANNE: Getting a coffee?

ANDREW: I can't drink coffee. What's the message?

LEANNE: Mr Perkins—he says traffic is expletive.

ANDREW: Who is 'Mr Perkins'?

LEANNE: Mr Perkins is your barrister. This will be over by the end of the day.

ANDREW: What are you talking about?

LEANNE: Your case. We are going to court. This is what we're here for.

> ANDREW's *phone rings.*

You didn't know?

ANDREW: I thought this was just another briefing.

LEANNE: Why would we schedule / another 'briefing' at the Magistrate's Court? Andrew, today is the day.

ANDREW: I dunno. I'm a musician. I'm not a bloody—am I an idiot? Am I a fuckwit? Really? Are we ready? / Fuck. This is it?

> LEANNE *receives a text message.*

LEANNE: Okay. This happens all the time. Melissa should have told you. / She should be informing you of the process. I will speak with her when this is over.

ANDREW: [*answering the phone*] Hello …? No. Fuck me, man. Five grand is my best and final … Sorry, mate—I've just got to go and get some justice.

> *He hangs up.*

LEANNE: Mr Perkins is in the building.

ANDREW: What does that mean?

LEANNE: Here we go.

> SIMON *turns up the volume gently—we are in the band room at Staccato. Posters on the walls from years of gigs. A whiteboard.*
>
> ANDREW *places his hands over his earbuds—listening to* SIMON's *iPod.* SIMON *is watching his reaction intently. Silence.*

## SCENE TWO: FUTURE-PROOFING

SIMON: How about that …? Good, isn't it …? Is it? Is it any good?

ANDREW: [*too loud*] This bass is fucking great!

SIMON: Ho—steady / on.

ANDREW: Very fucking cool.

    SIMON *takes one bud out—we can hear the sound.*

SIMON: Everyone / can—

ANDREW: Oh shit—sorry—

SIMON: It's fine. / Young people know swear words.

ANDREW: I forgot. Still getting used to—

SIMON: —the workplace?

ANDREW: Day job.

SIMON: Sure, man. Sure. Awesome, fantastic.

ANDREW: [*re: the music*] Where'd you find this?

SIMON: My daughter loves her. Uploaded it from iTunes.

ANDREW: Down. Doesn't matter.

SIMON: She records at home. Tiny town in the Land of the Long White Lord of the Rings. So many great Australian artists are Kiwis. Father sent a video of her to the record corporation and bang. She won a Granny.

ANDREW: Grammy.

SIMON: What was that?

ANDREW: Is she touring?

SIMON: No. Recording artist. So you love it?

ANDREW: It's good. [*Re: his phone*] I gotta get some shots for the Facebook page.

SIMON: Just good?

ANDREW: Bit derivative. Stand here and hold up this amp. Make it look like you're a roadie for Jackson Browne, you like his early stuff?

SIMON: Derivative of what?

ANDREW: What? I dunno. Fleetwood Mac, Prince, Michael Jackson. Madonna.

SIMON: So—derivative of popular music in general?

ANDREW: Put the amp on your shoulder.

SIMON: No. My assistant has a Pandora. How about this?

    *He offers a new recording.*

Debuted at number three on the Billabong charts.

ANDREW: Billboard.

    ANDREW *listens.*

SIMON: More in your wheelhouse …? Zippy. I'm no expert, but I know what other people like.

*Pause.*

Are you actually in a trance?

ANDREW: [*removing the buds*] Thanks for the tunes, Simon.

SIMON: Hated that too, huh?

ANDREW: Seriously, I think it's great somebody from the board is listening to contemporary stuff, if you know what I'm saying.

SIMON: Take it easy.

ANDREW: I've got to tell you I am very—excited.

SIMON: What's wrong?

ANDREW: Ideas for a new logo.

SIMON: What's the matter with the old one?

ANDREW: Frankly—it looks like a pile of birdshit.

SIMON: That was our competition winner.

ANDREW: That was the winner?

SIMON: Second place looked like a raging dildo.

ANDREW: [*laughing*] Schh—that is—you are a pistol.

SIMON: I'm deadly serious.

ANDREW: Well, the kids on the advisory panel wanna change it and I think you're going to fall in love with these / ideas.

SIMON: How do you know they want to change the logo?

ANDREW: I meet with them once a week.

SIMON: Who told you to do that?

ANDREW: It's in my job description.

SIMON: Carmel never did that.

ANDREW: Yeah, well. Hello? Not Carmel.

SIMON: / Where are your priorities? This place is falling apart. Something cool? What, like a food truck or something …? Hold on. Graffiti is illegal. It is a serious community concern, I've seen the polling on that.

ANDREW: They want the new logo to look like a record label or something cool. It's a great idea. They've got some mates—street artists, but they do more than tags—they do murals. Get this. They want the silhouette of our building to be the backdrop of the new Staccato visual presence—

SIMON: Drop it. Forget it.

ANDREW: But I think it's really clever.

SIMON: We have an existing logo—full stop.

ANDREW: Re-branding is—an actual thing—you know? In all honesty, I am finding it difficult to attract new members to the old pile of birdshit. Might be time to take a new pass at the image we are trying to project.

SIMON: Have they done a business case?

ANDREW: A what?

SIMON: Change is *expensive.*

ANDREW: It doesn't have to be. / The artists are working for free. It's a couple of business cards and the website—I don't see what the problem is.

SIMON: Get them to do a business case. A robust appraisal of the costs and benefits. Fiscal responsibility essential—

ANDREW: It's just a logo.

SIMON: The board will discuss it in the New Year.

ANDREW: Lemme show you some of these sketches.

SIMON: No. I actually dropped in to congratulate you.

ANDREW: Me?

SIMON: Great job on the AusCo application.

ANDREW: Oh. Man. / Thanks. That means a lot. We worked really hard on that document and yeah … thanks.

SIMON: Not at all. Scope. Vision. Just—too much. Enormous. 'Emerging Artists'. 'Regional-based'. Slipped in 'Diversity'. Tremendous.

ANDREW: Did you see the feedback forms we put in the support material?

SIMON: 'This music program is—dope!'

ANDREW: Fucking 'dope'—how about that?

SIMON: Dope is good, right?

ANDREW: Dope is great—

SIMON: Not wacky tobacky.

ANDREW: No, no, it's cool, / it's cool.

SIMON: And somebody wrote 'Staccato Rocks'… Did you write that one? Young people don't say 'rocks', do they? Sounds a little gen X to me.

ANDREW: Rock never dies.

SIMON: Disagree.

ANDREW: No. Rock lives.

SIMON: Confident?

ANDREW: Colin said it is unpredictable. Brandis is ripping the guts outta the AusCo. / But we are regional. That will help us.

SIMON: Yes, well … that's not exactly true. The Liberal Party is a great supporter of the arts. The minister is setting up Excellence Funding and that is really good for the regions and the opera. Excellence for everybody. Listen. Gotta dash. Running late for a sub-committee. But it's a great application. So. When we get the money—we can add it to the pot and move onto the next phase of refurbishment. We need that elevator fixed. Are the fairy lights in the milk crates?

ANDREW: What pot?

SIMON: Such an artist.

ANDREW: I'm actually Music Director and Co-CEO.

SIMON: On paper. Yes. / Six-month probation.

ANDREW: No. In reality. What is 'the pot'?

SIMON: I thought you were making a musician joke, but you … Let me explain.

> *He takes a whiteboard maker, uncaps it, and draws three circles on the board.*

What do you see here, Andy?

ANDREW: Three big balls. Like nuts. No, circles. Yes. No. What am I looking at?

SIMON: Grants. / Federal, State and Local.

ANDREW: Okay. I see that. Yes. Of course.

SIMON: These sacks of earned income all get put into one…

> *He draws a large circle around the three other circles.*

Big pot—to put the cash 'in'. Now. At the moment—Staccato exists inside a heritage-listed building. Which makes … [*writing and speaking at the same time*] 'Cap X = top priority'. When we get the money from AusCo—we can [*writing and speaking at the same time*] 'Fix … broken elevator.'

ANDREW: But the program money is not designated for capital works.

SIMON: / We talked about this at the Planning Day. My vineyard has huge expenses and lumpy income. Therefore I prepare for the worst and plan for the future. This is fiscal intelligence.

ANDREW: This money is specifically tied to the music activities for the members—we have to be specific in the way we spend it. Seriously? Is this how you do business?

JILL *arrives—she has one bud, laptop and skateboard.*

SIMON: Staccato is not-for-profit. We are essential to the cultural ecology and without our little roots in the landscape there will be an, an, an erosion that will become an unfillable sinkhole never to be filled. Our country is in danger of becoming a cultural cargo cult. Fully importing the next Split Enz. If we don't manage our balls and circles wisely there will be no future for the young people. Nothing. They will be dead. The young people will be dead, Ando. This is what you want, is it? You want to murder all of our emerging artists? You want the young people to die?

JILL: Busted.

SIMON: Who is?

JILL: Photoshop. Again. Can't do anything else today. I'm heading home.

ANDREW: Photoshop doesn't 'break'.

JILL: It's not letting me do it, Ando.

ANDREW: Do what?

JILL: Design. So I'll see you tomorrow—

SIMON: What are you designing?

JILL: Brochure for next year.

SIMON: Already?

JILL: He wants it done in a 'sap'.

SIMON: What's a sap?

JILL: It's another language. Like Japanese or some shit.

ANDREW: It's ASAP. / Just—accepted—management shorthand … Yes.

SIMON: Why are you designing a brochure when you don't know the outcome of the funding applications?

JILL: That's exactly what I was telling him.

SIMON: Oh-ah. No, no, no, stop work on the brochure I think.

ANDREW: [*to* JILL] You're not going home.

JILL: [*to* SIMON] He doesn't listen, that's his problem.

ANDREW: Nobody is stopping work on the brochure.

JILL: Tell that to Photoshop.

ANDREW: It can be fixed.

JILL: It's supposed to be intuitive.

SIMON: Ha. Nothing has been intuitive since the Bicentennial.

JILL: You need an expert.

ANDREW: I'll take a look under the hood in a minute.

JILL: What are you doing now?

ANDREW: We are actually in a meeting. Advisory kids came up with a new logo—

JILL: They're not kids, they're young people.

ANDREW: What's wrong with 'kids'?

JILL: Infantilism is oppression, perpetuated by the capitalist patriarchy.

SIMON: True dat.

ANDREW: [*to* JILL] Just lose the board and—get on with some other work.

JILL: Like what?

ANDREW: I don't know—the new database?

JILL: Ohhh, fucking hell! / Ando! You know I hate the new fucking database.

ANDREW: Jill. Don't say that— Yes. Yes. It has to be updated with data.

JILL: Your friggin' database was installed by trolls who play Minecraft.

ANDREW: We have got to pull it all together.

JILL: Triggers me so much.

SIMON: Triggers you?

JILL: I don't do data. / I work in the music industry. I am creative.

SIMON: 'Triggers me'… / that's a new one. Might use it.

ANDREW: Okay, okay. So what are you going to do for the rest of the day?

JILL: Get a coffee—do some shit on Pro Tools.

ANDREW: [*to* SIMON] I'm just gonna troubleshoot. Don't go anywhere, I wanna talk to you about some pathways. Leo from Mushroom called and he cannot wait to get involved, fair dinkum—he / is ready to burst.

SIMON: Leo? He's great … Burst …? Sounds messy.

> ANDREW *exits to work on the laptop. Music from* JILL'*s earbud.*

I like your hair like that …

JILL: [*re: the whiteboard*] What's this?

SIMON: Oh-ah. Something new.

SIMON *takes the loose bud from* JILL *and places it in his own ear.* JILL *is uncomfortable. He listens with his eyes closed. He puts a foot on an amplifier. A high piercing sound—tinnitus—drags us into the next scene.*

## SCENE THREE: TABLE OF CONTENTS

ANDREW: [*too loud*] Is this a corridor?

LEANNE: No. This is a fire escape. But. Good news? No fire. Not right now. Lucky us. Of course if there is a fire we are first in line. Half full, half empty—circuit is overcrowded, we grab any space we can—we booked this room weeks in advance.

ANDREW: It's not a room. / It's a fire escape. I'm meeting my barrister in—a—?

LEANNE: Today is all about being optimistic. Mr Perkins is on his way up.

ANDREW: Does he know which fire escape to come to?

LEANNE: Yes. Now. I must advise you to drop all reasonable expectations of everything.

ANDREW: Oh. Okay.

LEANNE: They will want to negotiate, but we don't know what that will look like until we get the offer and this is what they do. They will try and play mind games. Get in your head. Make you think you're guilty of something horrible. You're a bully, a beast, a boss from hell. Our contention is that they were negligent. Structured your dismissal. You have options. You can settle on the steps or we can walk into court together and Mr Perkins will run your case. Let the magistrate decide who is in the 'right'. Your decision—

ANDREW: That sounds really—HBO, but I have no idea how to determine what the— I didn't even know we were / doing this today.

LEANNE: Somebody really should have told you. But I feel good, I get a good feeling.

ANDREW: You get a good feeling?

LEANNE: Your board are amateurs, aren't they?

ANDREW: They actually sold their own building.

LEANNE: Who does that?

ANDREW *'s phone rings.*

ANDREW: How much is all this going to cost?

LEANNE: What's that? / No. This is no-win no-fee, that should have been explained. Of course there are running expenses, it's rare you have to reimburse out of your own pocket.

ANDREW: I don't have a regular income right now. All of my gear is on Gumtree. I mean all of it. I am struggling to pay the rent, I need whatever I can get my hands on, okay?

*He answers the phone.*

Hello?

*Lights back up on Staccato.*

SIMON: Who is it?

ANDREW: [*to the phone*] Fender, Maton and Gibson. With road cases … I'm not going lower than five grand … Fuck that, I can't do that.

*He hangs up.*

LEANNE: Turn it off.

ANDREW: I need the money.

LEANNE: We are dealing with your future.

JILL: Shanghai Susans.

SIMON *accidentally knocks the amplifier to the ground.*

## SCENE FOUR: ORG REVIEW

SIMON: I used to be an anarchist.

*Beat.*

Eat the rich.

JILL: Holy shit.

SIMON: Don't worry. Get a new one. Plant and equipment. How do you like him? Be honest. What's your verdict?

JILL: He listens to Red Hot Chilli Peppers in his car.

SIMON: Daggy. Right?

JILL: There is more to life than 'Blood Sugar Sex Magik'.

SIMON: Fur shuz.

JILL: He tries to talk like a CEO. 'Blue-sky, hit the ground running.'

SIMON: Gimme the quick and dirty.

JILL: What the fuck?

SIMON: Does 'Red Hot Chilli' know what he's talking about?

JILL: His Annual Program is a drive-by shooting.

SIMON: Okay. Is that good?

JILL: Too many targets. Not enough resources—

SIMON: / It's too much work, is it? Yes. It looked wayyy too much work to me. Yup … Yup … Yup … Nope. I know … Yes … It is completely—'over the top' for a small outfit like ours … I was voted down. I tried to reason—

JILL: If we actually do all the shit he's written up—all the concerts— the—the workshops and classes—all the shit in that spreadsheet? I mean, it would be fucking amazing, but we would need like two full-time administrators, a coupla producers, a hundred volunteers and actual—artists on staff.

SIMON: Artists on staff? Not going to happen.

JILL: I know. Right? The whole thing is sooo fucking Cold Chisel— so—twentieth century.

SIMON: Oh-ah. Hashtag awkward.

JILL: Soooo derivative.

SIMON: Hate that—

JILL: He thinks he's Michael fucking Gudinski, telling the funding bodies what he thinks they wanna hear. Our members don't wanna do classes, they just wanna fuck shit up.

SIMON: Right. Respect.

JILL: If we don't get the money there is no way we can deliver. And if we *do* get the money? I am *totally* joining a union.

SIMON: / Hold your horses—unions are crippling this country.

JILL: If he's such a gun bass player, what is he doing in a shithole like this?

SIMON: Yeah, well. He's not going to be here forever.

JILL: You just hired him—

> SIMON's *phone rings. It's in his pocket.*

SIMON: Almost finished his probation.

JILL: Andrew is on probation?

SIMON: *Everybody* has a probationary period.

JILL: Not me.

SIMON: Special case. Are you actually serious about threatening to join a union? Because we would fall apart without you.

JILL: I am serious about going on annual leave tomorrow night.

SIMON: Do you and I need an offsite meeting?

JILL: Are you gonna answer your pants?

> SIMON *retrieves his phone.*
>
> *Beat.*
>
> *Sends it to message bank.*

SIMON: Just Jodie.

JILL: Don't wanna talk to your wife?

SIMON: I'm—chillin'. In a meetin'. What are you doing for Christmas?

> SIMON'*s phone rings again. It's the same number.*

JILL: Got tickets for Falls for New Year's, I need an extra week off. Please?

SIMON: You're asking me?

JILL: Come on. You're The Man. Chairman of the board.

SIMON: Colin is our—GM.

JILL: Colin is in Thailand.

SIMON: Already?

JILL: I. Know. Don't you think our general manager should be overseeing the brochures? I mean, what does he get paid for? Just do it.

SIMON: Oh-ah. Why do you need an extra week?

JILL: See my father. He's sick. Probs terms.

SIMON: Speak to Colin when he gets back from Phuket.

JILL: Are you even listening / to me?

SIMON: Don't you have a portal here? We have a portal at my work.

JILL: I just told you my dad is like dying.

SIMON: So when are you going to Falls?

JILL: Are you calling me a liar?

SIMON: No. I'm not calling / you anything—

JILL: What gives you the right to tell me how to run my life?

SIMON: I'm not doing that—

JILL: I have ninety hours of TIL owing and I am gonna take what is mine.

> SIMON *grabs her wrist and offers her a present. It's a small box. He opens the box and reveals a set of earrings. Silence.*

SIMON: You're making me uncomfortable.

*Pause.*

What *kind* of a world are we living in when a middle-aged man cannot give a twenty-two-year-old girl a Christmas present …? I know you can't afford to buy nice things. I know you've got nothing. You deserve a reward for Christmas.

*Pause.*

I'm sorry if kindness is out of fashion. I teach my kids to give instead of receive. What is wrong with being—nice?

SIMON *forces the box onto* JILL *as* ANDREW *jogs in. Beat.*

We were just talking about Falls.

ANDREW: Boom! Jilly got tickets. Sold out in five hours.

SIMON: Yes. She told me all about it.

ANDREW: Hey! Great idea. Picture for Facebook! You on bass and Jill on drums. / Awesome—get on the drums and—

SIMON: Oh! No, no, no. No!

*Beat.*

Jill's juu-st running out the door. She's sick.

ANDREW: [*to* JILL] Are you okay?

*Pause.*

[*To* SIMON] Jill gets migraines.

*Silence.*

Pain management is very important, have you tried meditation?

JILL: Don't tell me what / to fucking do—

ANDREW: I'm just … Okay.

*Pause.*

Seriously. If you're sick, you may need to—lie down in a dark room.

JILL: Did you fix the Photoshop?

ANDREW: Trouble got shot.

JILL: What did you do?

ANDREW: Turned it off and on.

JILL: Surrounded by genius.

JILL *exits.*

SIMON: Hard worker. But she puts up walls, you know?

ANDREW: Did something happen in here?

SIMON: What? No. Why? Why? Why are you forcing her to use Photoshop to design a brochure that nobody is going to read because you don't even have the funding yet?

ANDREW: Did she tell you I am forcing her? / Is this about the brochure? Is she pissed off with me about the brochure, Simon? We've got to get to the kids before school breaks up. We have to go out before Christmas.

SIMON: My assistant uses InDesign for our internal newsletter and she is very arty. Okay. Question without notice. Migraine: Fact or fiction? I know people get migraines. But how many times a week? Has she seen her GP?

ANDREW: Yeah, I told her to do / that.

SIMON: Did she go?

ANDREW: She's her own person.

SIMON: Disagree. She is our employee. *Make* her go to the doctor. You're the boss. Get it documented. If she's claiming sick leave —she needs medical certificates. Believe it or not, this is an actual workplace. Not a drop-in centre for manic depressives.

> ANDREW *spots the newly broken amplifier.*

Jill smashed it. Temper tantrum.

ANDREW: I'll speak with her tomorrow—

SIMON: Why are you trying to humiliate her?

ANDREW: I'm not.

SIMON: You are creating a culture of fear.

ANDREW: Wait a second. We talked about culture of fear on the Planning Day. You remember? / I am setting 'achievable' standards.

SIMON: How could I forget? Leo was great! Charismatic. Imagine if somebody like him was working here? Amazing.

ANDREW: If Jill broke this / amplifier she has to—

SIMON: 'If' …? It was a violent outburst.

ANDREW: Okay. Let's write up an incident report. What happened?

SIMON: Nobody was injured—

ANDREW: No. But *what* happened?

> *Pause.*

I'll check the security footage.

SIMON: Send me the invoice. Move on.

ANDREW: You're going to pay for her bad temper?

SIMON: Who told you to start printing up bloody brochures?

ANDREW: Nobody / told me.

SIMON: Well, why are you doing it? Are you on the pipe?

ANDREW: We need our propaganda out there. We have to go into the school holidays with a bang! I've got Georgie and Tim from Inpress and NME running industry workshops, specifically for new bands. They are fucking amazing. They know publicity, business planning, they know contract negotiation and they are serious—social media gurus. Piston Biggie is doing five days on the decks.

SIMON: Piston what ? / Is that a gang, is this even legal ...? International?

ANDREW: 'DJing for Beginners and Intermediates', an international fucking legend of club and dance and trance and how cool is this?

SIMON: Sounds elitist.

ANDREW: Big is doing us a massive solid on his daily rate, / usually impossible to pin down—we are reeling in the big names.

SIMON: A solid? He's doing a 'solid' ...? Good God—

ANDREW: We have to get the good news into the streets! Seriously. Nobody will enrol if they don't know the program is happening. / Simon, trust me.

SIMON: Just—be honest. Will we get the AusCo money? Yes or no?

ANDREW: I don't know.

SIMON: This is starting to sound like a custard fuck.

ANDREW: I think you mean: 'cluster fuck'?

SIMON: How much are we spending on the Big Solid Piston?

ANDREW: You've lost me—

SIMON: It sounds like you're spending money we don't have.

ANDREW: It's all in the application.

SIMON: Okay. I'm breathing. Don't check the security footage because ... the cameras don't work. Okay?

*He draws a large 'X' on the board.*

They're fakes form the two-dollar shop because we can't afford proper security. This place is falling apart.

*He draws two more 'Xs'.*

Supposed to be accessible. Elevator is a deathtrap. It will cost a minimum of three hundred grand just to bring this place up to code. If we don't get the AusCo program money we will be—

*He writes 'Custard' under the Xs.*

ANDREW: 'Triple X Custard' …? What …? What are you writing about?

SIMON: We will be— [*Underlining 'Custard' frenetically*] —*custard fucked*. What's wrong with you? This bombsite is worth nothing but the land. We need to fix the elevator at a minimum. And this is all detailed in our—

*He writes: '(New) Strategic Plan'.*

Our—

*He writes: 'Mission Statement'.*

is totally—

*He writes: '21C'.*

That's management talk for 'twenty-first / century'

ANDREW: 'Twenty-first century', / yeah, I got that.

SIMON: Good. We all agree together.

ANDREW: Who is 'we'?

SIMON: Small working party. Reporting. To the board. They wanted to call it a 'sub-committee', but I'm already on one of those with the preselection, my diary would've been Auschwitz. So I pushed for 'Working Party'.

*SIMON underlines '(New) Strategic Plan'.*

ANDREW: You're talking about our core business. I should be at this party.

SIMON: Really? I mean—blah—finances. / Boring. Yuk.

ANDREW: Nah, nah, nah—I want to be in the room for this discussion.

SIMON: Do you really want to sit in a room with me and Barb and Councillor Brokeback Mountain? Come on. Is this the cool group? A lawyer, a bookkeeper and an arrhythmic chest infection?

ANDREW: You are talking about my Annual Program.

SIMON: Your Annual Program is our property.

ANDREW: I wrote the bloody thing. I set up all the artists and the teachers.

SIMON: If you put it in an email it belongs to us. Doesn't matter.

Working party is focusing on—

*He writes: 'Money', and underlines it.*

Should've put that in caps. Doesn't matter. 'Money' is 'focus' for all—

*He writes: 'NFPs'.*

That's not-for-profits.

*He underlines 'NFPs'.*

We have to futureproof our organisation from future funding cuts in the future. Debt and deficit is killing us. We have no definite income beyond today. Fairy lights? They have a bucket usually.

ANDREW: We have projected income. Workshops. Studio hire, box office, subscriptions, memberships, rooms for rent, special events and consultations.

SIMON: That is a projected projection.

ANDREW: You can't compare our business to a household budget.

SIMON: We—are a not-for-profit! And we are in a perilous position.

ANDREW: We can still be agile! / There is going to be a huge—upswing.

SIMON: Decisions have been made, Mr Gudinski. The working party has resolved that the best thing to do in the circumstances is—

*He writes: 'Sell Staccato'.*

This building is on the market.

ANDREW: You want to save Staccato by selling it?

SIMON: Yes. We sell—and ensure longevity for the organisation.

ANDREW: Where does the music go?

SIMON *tries to find space on the whiteboard—he ends up rubbing off half the writing that is up there and then writes 'ONLINE'.*

In caps.

SIMON: Totes caps.

*Pause.*

ANDREW: Okay. So—I'm not—I'm just—I'm just going to say this— okay?

SIMON: Depends what it is, that you are / trying to say.

ANDREW: What the fuck are you people thinking?! You hired me three months ago to run a music program / for young people.

SIMON: Listen, Red Hot Chilli. We hired you to write the grant application.

ANDREW: But now you're selling our bloody building! So what is the point of the funding application?

SIMON: This property is a deathtrap. It is our greatest liability. And I happen to think that young people deserve a little bit better than derelict, dangerous ex-government buildings, don't you? Oh no, that's right, you want to exterminate all the emerging artists in the world, don't you? Look at these walls.

ANDREW: / Living history. This is where the history is.

SIMON: Crumbling. Teenage hieroglyphics. Abhorrent. Unintelligible—

ANDREW: This is the heritage! We have to save these spaces or they are going to disappear—like the pubs—the clubs—the gigs—and, man! When I was their age we were playing in back rooms, basements, beer gardens—anywhere we could plug in. Drenched in beer and sweat and God knows what. One night we supported TISM at the Terminus Hotel and there were buckets in the corner collecting the perspiration streaming off the plasterboard ceiling, I mean it was utterly disgusting and completely fucking wonderful.

SIMON: Asbestos is everywhere. / Do you want a young person to come here and get seriously injured? Do you want somebody to contract mesothelioma?

ANDREW: My childhood was clad in fibro. This is nothing. This is nothing. We put 'em on the stage, we're not sending 'em down the mines.

SIMON: Australia has one of the highest rates in the world. It's a health and safety nightmare.

ANDREW: We can't 'go online'. I mean fuck. I mean fuck! Online. What is it?

SIMON: It's tomorrow. It's up there, Flea. It's in the broadband in the cloud. My firm hosted a Growing Community Leaders Enterprise and Business breakfast. The Dean from the university spoke and she was really— tall.Their School of Commerce, they deliver all of their modules online—they have students all over the world, Andrew. They have students in Hong Kong. Oh-ah. We must be nimble and online is the only way to guarantee a future for the good ship Staccato.

ANDREW: Disgaree.

SIMON: Okay. / I tried to give you the 'heads up'. You chose to ignore it. Where is the fairy bucket?!

ANDREW: How can you just slam me with this cyber shit? The AusCo don't know anything about it. Colin is gonna flip. He is gonna freak right the fuck out—

SIMON: Disagree! Colin. Fucking loves it.

ANDREW: When did you speak to Col?

SIMON: He's been helping us with the admin. He knows what I want.

ANDREW: What did you hire me for?

SIMON: You have great contacts.

ANDREW: Oh-ah. Now you do too.

> *Beat.*

SIMON: It doesn't have to end in acrimony.

ANDREW: End …? I'm not quitting. / I moved my life here. We bought a dog.

SIMON: Good. Good. Yup … You bought a dog?

ANDREW: Rescued a greyhound.

SIMON: What are you? A maniac? You're still on probation. Six months.

ANDREW: I thought that was a typo.

SIMON: No. It is a set period of time for us to determine whether or not we like you. What's happening with you and Jill? She was very angry about your Photoshop.

ANDREW: That isn't 'anger'. / Jill's fine. We understand each other.

SIMON: She broke the amplifier. Look. If a staff member is underperforming: set some measureables and get rid of her.

ANDREW: That your idea of team building?

SIMON: Linda suggested it.

ANDREW: Who's Linda?

SIMON: Our new Human Resources expert.

> *Beat.* SIMON *starts winding up a bundle of fairy lights.*

ANDREW: So is Linda working here now?

SIMON: No. Linda is on the board. HR is a gap. She comes highly recommended from State Government.

ANDREW: Arts and Culture?

SIMON: Nope.

ANDREW: Youth Services?

SIMON: Nope. Nope.

ANDREW: Major Events?

SIMON: Road and Maritime Services.

SIMON *keeps bundling.*

ANDREW: We need Philanthropic. / Development was identified at Planning Day.

SIMON: That's just a word. It's jargon. A fad. Linda wants to meet with you after your honeymoon.

ANDREW: How'd you know I'm getting married?

SIMON: Must have been the invitation I got in the mail. Oh-ah. That's right. Didn't get one of those. No rush. Soon as you get back. Informal. Offsite at the RMS.

ANDREW: What do you want me to prepare?

SIMON: Nothing. Just a catch-up.

ANDREW: Why don't we meet here? Hear some / music. Meet some members.

SIMON: Easier this way. Just a catch-up.

ANDREW: Did Linda really say that about Jill?

SIMON: No, Linda actually said that about you. Enjoy your honeymoon.

SIMON *smiles and exits, carrying the fairy lights.*

ANDREW *stands alone with the broken amplifier. Takes a battered guitar and a lead. Plugs it in and slams a chord—it rings with feedback. Hits a few more.*

JILL *enters, holding an A4 piece of paper.* ANDREW *doesn't see her at first. He continues to play. He sees* JILL.

*Pause. Last chord.*

JILL: Always sound better once you've kicked the shit out of them.

*Pause.*

What's wrong?

*Pause.*

You want some water or something?

ANDREW: [*re:* JILL'*s paper*] What's this?

JILL *hands* ANDREW *the paper.*

JILL: He's taking those lights home for Christmas, he does that every year.

ANDREW: [*reading*] 'Dear Ando, it has been nice meeting youse and hearing about the old school music business all the time. Good luck with your new Annual Program and everything. Cheers … Jill.'

JILL: My notice.

ANDREW: I can't accept this.

JILL: I'm not going to go back to fucken spellcheck it.

ANDREW: Are you quitting because of me?

JILL: Wow. Overwhelmed by compassion. Ta.

ANDREW: Is it because you broke this amplifier?

JILL: What the fuck?

ANDREW: It's no big deal. It doesn't have to escalate—

JILL: I did not fucking break this shitbox Pevey crap.

ANDREW: That's not what Simon says.

JILL: And you believe that fucker over me?

ANDREW: Fucker?

JILL: You kiss his arse so bad.

ANDREW: I respect his position.

JILL: You suck his dick like a bitch.

> *Back in the airlock,* PERKINS *arrives with a wheelie suitcase of documents.*

ANDREW: Sczhh. You need a holiday. / Lie in the sun. Read a book.

JILL: I hate this place. He is a skull-fucking / cunt.

ANDREW: Oh—okay. Yup.

JILL: That bag of pus is a goddamned—

> *She writes 'Liar' on the whiteboard, drops the pen and exits.*

## SCENE FIVE: STRENGTHS, WEAKNESSES, OPPORTUNITIES & THREATS

LEANNE: This is Mr Perkins.

PERKINS: Andrew!

ANDREW: Great—just—just—gimme a second.

*SCENE SIX: STAFFING NEEDS*

*Onstage at Staccato. Lights on the deck.* JILL *is testing and tagging.*

ANDREW: Jill. I'm the boss. I'm serious. I refuse to accept your resignation.

JILL: These old PAR cans are crap.

ANDREW: You actually don't give me the impression of somebody who is trying to leave the music business.

JILL: Does somebody have to get killed before they're replaced with LEDs?

ANDREW: Do you sing?

JILL: Do I what?

ANDREW: Sing. Do you sing? With your voice.

JILL: My sister is the singer.

> *She keeps working.*

ANDREW: What's her name?

JILL: She's not a puppy.

> *She keeps working.*

ANDREW: You play an instrument?

JILL: You know what I do. I work the front desk and I fuck up the brochures.

ANDREW: I don't think this is really why you wanna quit, is it—?

JILL: What the fuck is a 'CoB'? Huh? What is that even supposed to mean? 'CoB'. Nobody ever said that to me before you got here. Carmel never said it. Colin never says it. 'CoB' You sound like a fucking goose. 'CoB' 'CoB' … 'CooooBBB' … You make up words to make people feel like they are fucking failures, that's what you do. 'CoB'. 'CooooBBBB'. You're so full of shit, it's coming out of your mouth.

ANDREW: Do you mean C.O.B?

JILL: / What the fuck does that mean?

ANDREW: 'Close of Business'.

JILL: Did you swallow a management calendar or something?

ANDREW: I'm not a manager.

JILL: Correct.

ANDREW: I'm sorry. I am a musician.

JILL: What are you doing here?

ANDREW: I applied because I couldn't play live anymore and … I saw this job advertised and I didn't think I had a chance … but they hired me. Still not sure why. But. Writing the Annual Program—we have a chance to … And now … you're quitting? Because I sound like a goose …? Gimme a break. I don't know the lingo.

JILL: 'Lingo' … ? / O.M.G.

ANDREW: I have no idea how a Co-CEO is supposed to talk. I read up on all the jargon for the interview. I am improvising. Still on my L-plates. Hand on heart. This is my first full-time job. Serious. Mind blown? I'm hangin' on with both hands.

JILL: You never had a proper job before?

ANDREW: Never. Well. I played music.

JILL: But how'd you pay the rent?

ANDREW: Yeah. No. I was pretty good. But played too loud too long. Tinnitus. Ringing in my ears and it gets bad with loud noises …

JILL: You can't drink coffee or alcohol. Worse with stress. Like a migraine.

ANDREW: That's right. How'd you know?

JILL: I've got friends who suffer.

ANDREW: No way.

JILL: We measure all our shows now, but back in the day … You should try yoga and meditation. That can work.

ANDREW: Yeah, yeah. I know. Got to make time.

JILL: They are getting rid of you.

ANDREW: What?

JILL: Didn't know that?

ANDREW: No.

JILL: Simon is going to dump you at the end of your probation.

ANDREW: No. No way. I think you're confused. Yeah. No. I'm getting married. He knows I need this job. I have / a contract—

JILL: Ando … What was Simon doing in here?

ANDREW: Fairy lights. That's about it. And—he actually came in to say, 'Well done, to everyone, on the application'. Just a 'catch-up'. That's it.

JILL: 'Catch-up' is code for 'We're fucking you over' … But you'd know that from your management research. Right?

ANDREW: It's not a code. It's words. Just jargon. It's nothing to worry about.

JILL: I was just getting to know you, too.

ANDREW: Hey. I am here for the long haul.

JILL: That's what Carmel said.

ANDREW: What happened to Carmel?

JILL: The board did a review of the Org Structure. Re-named her position. She had to reapply and you got the job. I quit.

ANDREW: You can't quit. You're the only person here who likes music.

JILL: Andrew! This pressure is killing me.

ANDREW: What pressure?

JILL: You! You bring it big time! You changed everything!

ANDREW: No, I haven't—

JILL: But you like—want the brochure done—!

ANDREW: / Yes.

JILL: By a certain time and date!

ANDREW: Yes.

JILL: Well, I'm not used to this kind of pressure.

ANDREW: Is the pressure giving you migraines?

JILL: I do not get migraines.

ANDREW: You told me you were getting / migraines.

JILL: I lied. I lied.

> *Pause.*

I lie.

ANDREW: What happened to the amplifier?

JILL: Simon said he used to be an 'anarchist'.

ANDREW: Do you know what an anarchist is?

JILL: I know what Simon is.

> *Silence.*

ANDREW: Who are you listening to?

> JILL *puts the earbuds near* ANDREW's *ears—but not in them.*

[*Listening*] Red wine and cigarettes. Who is she?

JILL: My sister.

*They both listen.*

ANDREW: This bass player sounds like Carol Kaye.

JILL: You know Carol Kaye?

ANDREW: Carol Kaye is Motown. The bass in everything.

*He listens.*

JILL: What do you think of Gail Ann Dorsey?

ANDREW: She's the … / with David Bowie?

JILL: She played with Bowie, that's right. Smooth and solid.

ANDREW: Without being flashy.

JILL: Exceptional.

ANDREW: Oh, this. This one—reminds me of Kim Deal.

JILL: Kim Deal? No way.

ANDREW: You know her?

JILL: Man, I love The Pixies.

ANDREW: You're too young to love The Pixies.

JILL: I know good shit when I hear good shit. But that doesn't sound
like Kim Deal. You're confused old man.

ANDREW: Old man?

JILL: Kim Deal is history. This is tomorrow.

ANDREW: Who am I listening to?

JILL: Shanghai Susans.

ANDREW: Good demo.

JILL: Thanks.

ANDREW: You made this?

JILL: In my bedroom and I mixed it on the Pro Tools in here at work.

*She cuts the sound—silence.*

I want to be a producer.

ANDREW: You want to produce?

JILL: So what?

ANDREW: So nothing—so what else have you got?

JILL *selects another track.*

JILL: Okay?

ANDREW: Assault and battery.

JILL: Arctic Park.

ANDREW: Good shit.

JILL: *Très* good shit. They meet at the station. They pretend they're in the subways in Brooklyn or something urban. They tag the place up and I took a field recorder and got them to do some rhymes, mixed it with the sound of the trains and the traffic in the rain and ... He needs to slow down—but he's getting better.

ANDREW: Do your bands play at Staccato?

JILL: Nah.

ANDREW: Why not?

JILL: They're artists. This place is for kids.

ANDREW: 'Young people'.

JILL: No. They want kids in here. Ever since Simon has been the boss.

ANDREW: He's the Chair, he's not the boss.

JILL: He loves the pile of birdshit. Thinks it looks like a treble clef.

ANDREW: Holy fuck.

JILL: His dream is to get the whole world to stream Celine Dion forever.

ANDREW: Okay. Stop work on the brochure.

JILL: I already quit—

ANDREW: Let's do something amazing.

JILL: They're selling Staccato.

ANDREW: How'd you know that?

JILL: I am fluent in whiteboard.

ANDREW: Okay.

JILL: Good luck.

ANDREW: You can't fucking quit, Jill.

JILL: Just watch me.

ANDREW: Music keeps you breathing.

JILL: What the fuck?

ANDREW: You won't survive a week without Staccato.

JILL: Look. I don't even know you.

ANDREW: You got Pro Tools at home, have you?

JILL: I don't come here for the apps, Andrew.

ANDREW: Why *do* you come to work? Here? Early. Every day. What's in it for you?

JILL: The money.

ANDREW: Don't buy it. No. None of us do this for / the money.

JILL: I'm just telling you the way it is for me.

ANDREW: Okay. Imagine Staccato doesn't exist. How do you feel about that?

JILL: I don't care.

ANDREW: You lie. You're a liar.

JILL: I don't care.

ANDREW: Music makes me.

> *Beat.*

Makes me cry and shake—makes me wail. I can't—When I hear Iggy and the Stooges—fuck me—I am a … not because it's beautiful, but because it is so bloody. 'Lust for Life' … Shit. You know what I mean. We are the dogs. Transponders.

> *Pause.*

You can leave now. But you'll be back. You've done the deal.

PERKINS: You are the plaintiff.

ANDREW: When did you realise you'd die without music in your life?

PERKINS: And this is your case! /

## SCENE SEVEN: VISION STATEMENT

PERKINS: Not many people make it past conciliation. But you did. You have a matter of 'genuine' dispute. Well done. But beware. The System is designed to discourage individuals from taking action. It is constructed to wear / you down.

LEANNE: Their strategy is to confuse and fatigue the plaintiff.

ANDREW: You make it sound like a conspiracy.

LEANNE: It is.

PERKINS: How many forms have you filled in—?

ANDREW: Hundreds.

PERKINS: How'd that go for you?

ANDREW: Nothing happened.

LEANNE: Exactly—

PERKINS: Now, as your barrister I take instructions from you. This is your case and I want to win.

ANDREW: What do you need from me? / What can I do?

PERKINS: Facts. I need all the facts.

ANDREW: You've got / copies of my notes and documents. That's right, isn't it?

LEANNE: All the notes. / All the depositions and the witness statements. Yes.

PERKINS: Yes. Doctors' reports. And your narrative is a predictable chain of events, Fair Work—Work Safe—the Ombudsman—the local council. You met with the local council—the Arts Department—some of them were on your board, weren't they? They knew what was happening in their building.

LEANNE: Of course they knew. They are complicit.

ANDREW: So what do we do?

PERKINS: And so we fight. Thank God for your union, hey?

*The sound of tinnitus coming from a long way away.*

LEANNE: What's the matter …? What's wrong …? You're not going to start waving your arms again, are you? You are here. / You are alive.

PERKINS: I am ready for your instruction!

## SCENE EIGHT: FACTS AND FIGURES

ANDREW: We are gonna wake the dead! Backlines everywhere. PAs in every room. Just blast away all day and night. Decks upstairs—Shanghai Susans on the main stage, Arctic Park on the balcony over the street after midnight. We have to show this city what is beating inside these walls!

JILL: The board won't come. / They fucking hate rock and hip-hop and—there are already so many festivals out there.

ANDREW: We don't want them in here—we want the new faces—with the new sounds. This is different.

JILL: What's the budget?

ANDREW: If we build it—the box office will come! / My hair is standing on end, come on—we came here for a reason. I can't walk away without making some noise. Let's set this place on fire.

JILL: You can't just rely on ticket sales. We need sponsors, if we do this, we have to make it fucking good! My sister and I used to organise the Sunday afternoons. It was steaming. Those gigs were … great. Simple. Bands on the stage and drinks in the foyer. We just wanted to be in the room.

ANDREW: This room?

JILL: This room. This crowded dance floor. Crash barriers. Screaming our lungs out. Crowd-surfing. Getting carried all the way to the back and then crawling through the legs—get up the front. Do it all again. The floor is bouncing. Actually bending. It's so loud, nobody can hear. So loud you don't even know if it is your laughter. Your voice. Your life. One body. One soul. A snake. Smashing and bleeding and—not even realising you're cut until you go home. In here—it didn't hurt so much. Not for a couple of hours. We lived for the weekend. If you're going to do this … do it properly … Festoon lights and food trucks. Outdoor table tennis. A whole two days, no—three days and nights of new music.

ANDREW: And all of it programmed by you.

JILL: Hold it a second—

ANDREW: You wanna be a producer? I'll teach you everything I know. Let's turn this place up to—

*He writes '11' on the board.*

JILL: What's double 'I' mean?

ANDREW: No, that's eleven. [*Heavily underlining on the board*] 'Eleven'.

*He drops the whiteboard marker. When it hits the floor it sounds like a guitar lead getting plugged into an amplifier.*

Real life is in demand!

*The buzz of an amp coming to life.*

This summer. I believe … I can see it. Core business equals 'excitement'! Come on!

*Tambourine and kick drum.*

Local groups! New music! Staffing needs? Artists who deserve attention! Gimme some bass and B3 Hammond! Yeah!

*Bass and B3 Hammond organ.*

My scoping vision for our future? Arse-kicking live music comes back to Staccato. How the fuck does this sound?

JILL: Could be shit.

*Tom-tom roll and bass kicks in.*

ANDREW: A sonic exorcism! A music-led recovery! Festival of youth music called: 'Summer Fun'!

JILL: What the fuck is that? / 'Summer fucking Fun'?

*Two guitars.*

ANDREW: First draft. Come on—it's outdoors—in the sunlight.

JILL: I'm not programming some shitbag show called 'Summer Fun'. It's gotta sound like the vibe you wanna bring.

ANDREW: 'Reverberation'!

JILL: Are you trying to trigger me?

ANDREW: 'Sound Check'.

JILL: The 'Sound Check' Festival …?

ANDREW: I've heard worse. Until we find the right name, let's just call it our …

JILL: 'Strategic Plan.'

ANDREW: Oh. That's good … It is subversive. It is zeitgeist! It is—

JILL: Fucking terrifying—

ANDREW: Let's go!

> *Long vocal and full band and tinnitus and then—lights flash to blinders and darkness.*
>
> *Music in the darkness.*

## SCENE NINE: MISSION STATEMENT

*After the honeymoon. Hot January.*

*Gentle State Government phones from adjoining offices ring at random throughout this scene.*

*Grey lights up on a nondescript meeting room at the Road Traffic Authority. There is a circular table, the same roller chairs and a water cooler. A bin and a large conference flip board with permanent markers. No windows.*

*LINDA is alone in the space. She claps her hands. The lights come on. She is making final adjustments to the placement of the items in the room. She is almost rehearsing meeting ANDREW.*

*ANDREW appears in the room, wearing Hawaiian shirt and shorts.*

LINDA: How did you get in here?

ANDREW: I think I'm supposed to be here—

LINDA: Nobody is supposed to be here.

ANDREW: No—the young woman—

LINDA: Calm down.

ANDREW: Linda?

LINDA: Stand back.

ANDREW: No—

LINDA: I know jiujitsu.

ANDREW: We are supposed to be meeting today.

LINDA: How do you know my name?

ANDREW: I'm Andrew.

LINDA: I can see your legs.

ANDREW: Yes—it's hot outside.

LINDA: The air is cool inside—

ANDREW: We don't have air conditioning at Staccato.

LINDA: Why not?

ANDREW: We're—a not-for-profit.

LINDA: Yes, I know. I'm on the board.

ANDREW: You are Linda.

LINDA: Correct.

ANDREW: Should we—shake hands?

LINDA: Are you Hawaiian?

ANDREW: No.

LINDA: Where did you get your shirt?

ANDREW: Newtown …

> LINDA *offers her hand.*

LINDA: Andrew—we've gotten off on the wrong foot—let's shake hands.

> *They shake hands.*

Normally they ring to tell me there is a visitor, it's a security thing—did you sign in?

ANDREW: I signed in.

LINDA: Nothing personal.

ANDREW: No.

LINDA: Just keeping the public away from the management. Safety first. So you're the musician.

ANDREW: Director of Music. Co-CEO.

LINDA: Simon said you're an old musician.

ANDREW: Silly Simon.

> *Lights go to grey.* LINDA *moves like Peter Garrett. Lights back on.*

LINDA: What instrument did you used to play?

ANDREW: I still play bass. Guitar. Keyboards. Whatever.

LINDA: But now you've got a real job. We employ you.

ANDREW: Yes. But I still play every now and then. It's kind of important. It gives the young people an indication of—pathways.

LINDA: So they end up like you?

ANDREW: How did you get involved with the board?

LINDA: We know each other. He's going to be a powerful local member.

ANDREW: Simon's going to be a politician?

LINDA: At last. Somebody to vote for.

ANDREW: What kind of music do you like?

LINDA: No. My calling is Human Resources.

ANDREW: Looks like it's—pretty loud.

LINDA: Do you know anything about building roads? No. And yet you use them every day. Isn't that fascinating? So many people in the community simply forget just how often they use roads. Taxi drivers don't. Uber do. Did Simon ride with you?

ANDREW: He said he'd meet me here.

LINDA: Colin is nice. Soft hands. He used to be a middle-distance runner.

ANDREW: Didn't know that.

LINDA: I compete in triathlons. I keep going until I vomit. Ever pushed yourself to that point of exhaustion?

ANDREW: I've always wanted to run a marathon.

LINDA: What's stopping you?

> *Beat.*

I've brought this big notepad thing in. We may not even use it, but I think it could be good if we want to make some notes. Big notes.

ANDREW: This is just a catch-up / right?

LINDA: Water? It is essential to rehydrate. Wait here. I'll be back in no time.

> LINDA *exits.* ANDREW *checks his phone. Straightens his shirt. Sits. Finds the most casual pose he can establish. There is a low-pitched hum in the room. Lights go to grey.*

> SIMON *enters.* SIMON *has his arm in a sling. Lights flick on.* SIMON *is surprised to see* ANDREW *in the room.*

SIMON: Did you do that?

ANDREW: I don't know— What happened [*to your arm*]?

SIMON: Oh … a dog was unleashed.

ANDREW: When did you get back?

SIMON: I just took the public holidays. Are we in the right room?

ANDREW: This is where she brought me.

SIMON: Young woman at the front? Looks like a cordless phone—her face—you know? [*Regarding the room*] Inspirational.

ANDREW: You ever run a marathon?

SIMON: What for?

ANDREW: There's a fire outside.

SIMON: Didn't see it.

ANDREW: The sky is black.

SIMON: Disagree.

ANDREW: Nice cufflink.

SIMON: Jodie. Spends my money like a Doomsday Prepper. Competing with her sister. Finds shiny things—leaves them on my dressing table. I would shoot myself in the mouth if I had to come in here every day.

ANDREW: Me too.

SIMON: You think about that sort of thing a lot?

ANDREW: No.

SIMON: So why did you say it?

ANDREW: I thought you were joking.

SIMON: Jokes.

> SIMON *sits at the table and makes a note—completes his writing and looks* ANDREW *in the eye. Pause.* SIMON *gets a text message. Finds his spectacles. Puts them on and accesses the message. Smiles at what he reads. Types a reply with his index finger.*

Bought myself a Christmas present. Jag. XER Sport. [*Putting his spectacles away*] Gotta pay the rego. Might just duck out and … You don't mind, do you …?

> *Pause.*

No. No … I'm joking.

> *Pause.*

Pay on the way out. This won't take long. Linda's got a few things she wants to go through. Colin back on deck?

ANDREW: Next week.

SIMON: Nice break.
ANDREW: Lucky for some.
SIMON: He works long hours. Lot of time in lieu banked up.
ANDREW: We *all* work long / hours, Simon.
SIMON: Yes alright, so what's the problem?
ANDREW: No problem. It just makes it difficult.
SIMON: You've got Jill. Is she happy? Is Jill happy?
ANDREW: Yes.
SIMON: Did you give her the extra week off?
ANDREW: She doesn't want the extra week off.
SIMON: Did her father die this time?
ANDREW: She didn't say anything.
SIMON: No mention of a dead father?

> *Lights to grey.*

ANDREW: She's working on the festival, new lease on life.
SIMON: And where is the budget for this fiesta coming from?
ANDREW: It's selling really well—
SIMON: But where's the budget line?
ANDREW: Do you have a problem with me?
SIMON: Do you have a problem with me?
ANDREW: I asked first.
SIMON: Do you have a problem with Colin?
ANDREW: No.
SIMON: That's not what Colin said.

> LINDA *enters with folders and water bottles—lights on.*

LINDA: It's a / madhouse!
SIMON: Bloody hell. That's an entrance.
LINDA: Start of the year, always the same, everybody covering for
    everybody else, don't know why they put me in charge, but they
    did, so you found the room okay—?
SIMON: / Yes. Of course. Congratulations.
ANDREW: No worries.
LINDA: Thanks for coming cross-town, Andy. My calendar! Terrifying.
SIMON: Ando says they're hopelessly understaffed.
LINDA: Hopelessly?
SIMON: Everybody's on holidays apparently.

ANDREW: / Linda—really—it's fine.

SIMON: They're under siege. Did you see the shirt?

LINDA: Yes.

SIMON: Hear about the bushfire?

LINDA: The what?

SIMON: Ando says it's out of control. We're all going to die.

LINDA: We're not going to die, are we, Andy?

ANDREW: Hope not.

SIMON: Can we get that in writing?

LINDA: Said the lawyer.

> *She laughs.* SIMON *watches her like he's observing sperm. Beat.*

Hawaiian.

ANDREW: There *really* is a fire … Five, six trucks …The sky is black. Do you want to come outside / and have a look?

SIMON: Is that what you want us to do? Go and look at a bushfire?

LINDA: As a group? Like a band?

SIMON: Take a selfie for Facey?

ANDREW: No.

LINDA: Good, because my morning is gridlocked. Shall we get this underway? Ready, set, go! But before we begin I think we'd all like to show our respect and acknowledge the traditional custodians of this land, of elders past and present, on which this event takes place.

SIMON: Amen.

LINDA: Amen?

SIMON: Reflex action.

ANDREW: Is this an event?

SIMON: You don't want to acknowledge the original Australians, Ando?

ANDREW: Yeah, no, no, yes.

SIMON: See …? Doesn't take much. Reconciliation.

LINDA: A daily action.

SIMON: If my phone rings, I have to take it.

LINDA: Put it on silent.

SIMON: Can you do that?

LINDA: What kind is it?

SIMON: It's a smartphone.

> LINDA *takes* SIMON*'s phone and tries to put it on silent. Drops the phone on the table in a flourish of success.*

LINDA: Annnd—that's how we roll at the RMS.

SIMON: You'll have to show me what you pushed.

LINDA: Like your cufflink.

SIMON: Christmas.

LINDA: How's Jodie?

SIMON: Great. Her family—just wonderful. Father has a garage full of Lambos and a little Maserati. Big celebration. Quality people. We had them all down to the vineyard and they brought their pets … You know? Played tennis. Not with the animals, but you know? There was an incident and it is healing. You? Yours? Massive?

LINDA: Mum's got a new boyfriend.

SIMON: What's he do?

LINDA: Final year Law at UTS.

SIMON: Good God.

LINDA: I know. Showed me his student card.

SIMON: UTS.

> *Beat.*

LINDA: Oh, you! I love it! So … Andy. How are you? Big year ahead!

ANDREW: Think so.

LINDA: Not sure what you're doing?

ANDREW: Yeah, no. The board signed off on the Annual Program.

SIMON: Lot of plans.

ANDREW: It's our Annual Program.

LINDA: These planned activities?

ANDREW: The Annual Program is what we're doing in order for us to achieve the goals and objectives outlined in your Strategic Plan.

LINDA: 'Outcomes cannot exist until a plan has been executed.'

> SIMON *takes his pen and writes something.*

Haven't heard that one before?

SIMON: No. Just got a little Jag. Thought of a new number plate.

LINDA: Right.

SIMON: No, it was good—I was joking! It's great … 'Outcomes—are plans'?

LINDA: 'Outcomes cannot exist until a plan / has been executed.'

SIMON: '… until a plan has been executed' … Who said that?

LINDA: My desk calendar. Mum gave it to me for Christmas.

ANDREW: Your mother gave you a desk calendar?

LINDA: Yes.

SIMON: Something you can use every day.

> *Pause.*

Thank you.

> LINDA *starts laughing.*

LINDA: Oh—I can never tell with you, Simon.

SIMON: At uni I could quote whole scenes of 'Monty Python' … I can't now. Used to have a photographic memory. They called me 'Nikon'. After the camera. It wasn't racist. It was a term of affection. What'd they call you at university, Andrew?

ANDREW: I didn't go to university.

SIMON: Oh, that's right. I forgot.

LINDA: [*to* ANDREW] So. All funded? These plans of yours.

ANDREW: They're not plans of *mine*, Linda.

LINDA: But you are proud of this funding application—document—thing?

ANDREW: It is going to be a National Benchmark.

LINDA: And you're happy with that?

ANDREW: Aren't you?

LINDA: This delivery schedule—wow. Lot of KPIs to hit in six months. Significant increase in metrics for everybody. Is that a new concern?

SIMON: Why do you keep changing the goalposts?

ANDREW: How am I doing that?

LINDA: Forcing a junior employee to produce a whole festival by herself.

ANDREW: She has been looking for a challenge for some time.

SIMON: Sounds like you're setting her up to fail.

ANDREW: She's not going to fail.

LINDA: No specific budget allocation. She doesn't need the extra pressure.

ANDREW: Who told you that?

LINDA: Does it matter?

ANDREW: I'm not *setting* anybody up. I don't do that.

SIMON: No. You rescue dogs.

ANDREW: Sorry. Can I confirm—what exactly is this meeting about?

LINDA: Catch-up. Just a catch-up.

ANDREW: He told me there was nothing to prepare.

SIMON: Calm down.

LINDA: Your probation is almost up.

ANDREW: So—this is my review? / Is this my review?

LINDA: You've got this massive focus on live music.

ANDREW: Yes. Well, music is our—reason for being.

LINDA: Are we comfortable with that?

ANDREW: It is in the original Strategic Plan that was written by us—by all of us at Planning Day. And so, we are kicking this New Year off with—the Second City Festival.

SIMON: What's your point?

ANDREW: You cannot sell our building and you will not go online.

SIMON: 'Our' building?

LINDA: That's not on the agenda for this meeting—

ANDREW: Well, the staff think it needs to be.

SIMON: 'The staff'?

ANDREW: That's right.

SIMON: Acting in isolation from the membership base. Are we, Drewster?

LINDA: Why did you force Jill to write a resignation letter?

SIMON: Yes, why did you do that?

ANDREW: I didn't force anybody to write anything.

SIMON: Avoiding the question.

ANDREW: Jill handed me a resignation letter and I refused to accept it.

LINDA: You refused?

ANDREW: She doesn't want to resign because of me.

LINDA: That's what you think?

ANDREW: That's what I know.

SIMON: You don't know anything about her.

ANDREW: She came to my wedding.

SIMON: One of the lucky few to get an invitation.

> *Lights snap to grey.* LINDA *waves her arms like Peter Garrett.*
> *Lights back on.*

LINDA: Her work schedule is punishing.

SIMON: 'Punishing'—

ANDREW: Take it / easy.

LINDA: Do the staff agree to the proposed increase in the workload?

ANDREW: Why are you so fixated on the workload?

SIMON: Crikey.

LINDA: Fixated?

SIMON: Heard that.

LINDA: You *did* consult with staff about heavier workloads, right?

ANDREW: We have been talking about change for / six months.

LINDA: That's not my question.

ANDREW: Did I consult with them? Personally? No. I don't do the rosters—that's Colin's gig.

LINDA: Did you discuss it with Colin?

SIMON: How does Colin feel about the festival?

ANDREW: He doesn't know about it. He's in Thailand.

LINDA: So—you just created this new workload off your own bat?

ANDREW: I am not going to call him in Thailand to get his 'approval'. He's on holidays.

LINDA: And you resent that?

SIMON: Sounds jealous.

LINDA: How does Jill feel about the Annual Program?

ANDREW: Jill?

SIMON: Jill.

ANDREW: Specifically Jill?

SIMON: Have you sought out feedback on the Annual Program with Jill?

ANDREW: Jill's fine.

SIMON: We don't want to lose Jill.

ANDREW: No, I know you don't want to lose Jill.

LINDA: Jill—is on the front desk, right?

SIMON: Yes—

ANDREW: And producing the festival, doing amazing work.

LINDA: Sounds like you're outsourcing your own job?

ANDREW: I am 'mentoring' her through 'the process' and giving her plenty of 'latitude' to create a 'pathway' for 'emerging artists' in 'the regions'. I know. I am Satan, I'm sorry.

LINDA: Did you consult with her individually on the grant application?

ANDREW: No.

LINDA: But 'Satan' is throwing this major / event on her plate? But this is additional work, this is unbudgeted activity and completely impulsive.

ANDREW: I don't accept that. Col and I wrote the application together.

The board signed off on it. He went on holidays. Then the board changed your mind and decided you wanted to sell off / the biggest asset—

LINDA: I might just stop you there— The board didn't 'sign off' on anything.

ANDREW: Yes. They did. They approved it. / Simon? You approved it.

LINDA: Andy, Andy … you're referencing the November meeting?

ANDREW: The last board meeting of the year. Yes.

LINDA: My first meeting was in December. In camera.

SIMON: While you were still on your honeymoon.

ANDREW: What was on the agenda?

SIMON: Range of topics. Can you smell smoke?

ANDREW: Were you talking about me?

SIMON: Don't be paranoid.

LINDA: A Strategic Plan is an *organic* document. It must be organic. It is a road map to inform our future. Like the Koran. No good sitting on a dusty shelf gathering—dust. The board sets the direction, Andy. We have to stay on trend or we are dead. We do not need a new logo and we cannot afford this music 'festival'.

   *Lights go to grey.*

ANDREW: You talked about Second City in the December meeting?

SIMON: And the need for more frequent meetings.

ANDREW: Without me—and without our General Manager?

SIMON: No. Colin. Took the minutes.

ANDREW: You just said it was in camera.

SIMON: It was actually in the board room. He Skyped it in.

ANDREW: He Skyped from Thailand to take minutes …? I don't believe that for a … On Skype? From Phuket? To take minutes?!

   *Beat.* LINDA *waves her arms like Peter Garrett. Lights back on.*

LINDA: Have you heard of the phrase 'emotional intelligence', Andrew?

ANDREW: You know what? I have to get back to work.

LINDA: No. You've got time.

ANDREW: We have a festival to deliver.

LINDA: Andy—

ANDREW: Lindy?—

SIMON: No need for that—

LINDA: On a scale of one to ten—with ten being extremely competent and one being disastrous—how would you rate your emotional intelligence?

ANDREW: I've never reflected on my 'emotional intelligence' before today, Linda.

SIMON: So … five?

ANDREW: No.

SIMON: Six?

ANDREW: I would have / said …

LINDA: Seven?

ANDREW: Nine point eight.

SIMON: No way.

ANDREW: Seven point five.

SIMON: Sold. Couldn't help myself.

ANDREW: You *told* me this was 'just a catch-up'.

LINDA: You were informed that you have nothing to worry about. Correct?

ANDREW: / 'Worry'? Jesus. That's a word.

LINDA: How do you deal with conflict, Andy?

ANDREW: It depends on how I'm being ambushed.

LINDA: / You think we're trying to ambush you?

SIMON: You think this is an ambush?

LINDA: Describe for me—

SIMON: For us—

LINDA: —your approach to conflict resolution.

ANDREW: What if I don't want to do that?

LINDA: That's fine. I'll just write: 'Refuses to provide a response'.

ANDREW: What's the conflict about?

LINDA: Does it matter?

ANDREW: Who's involved?

LINDA: Why do you treat people differently?

ANDREW: I don't.

SIMON: Why does it matter who's involved in the dispute?

ANDREW: What is the *cause* of the dispute?

LINDA: Time in lieu. That's a huge issue right now.

SIMON: We cannot afford to carry that liability.

LINDA: So—there is a dispute between Colin and—one of the casuals.

The casual wants extra hours. Colin doesn't want to give them. What do you do?

ANDREW: Nothing. Not my job.

LINDA: But how do you resolve the issue?

ANDREW: The General Manager is in charge of the TIL. This is his area.

LINDA: You don't help him?

ANDREW: I don't / interfere.

LINDA: Not a team player?

ANDREW: I am not a micromanager.

LINDA: So, you think you're his manager?

ANDREW: We are colleagues.

LINDA: You don't want to help your colleagues, Andy?

ANDREW: Your scenario demonstrates a fundamental misunderstanding of our core business.

LINDA: Which is what?

ANDREW: What?

LINDA: What is our core business? In your opinion?

ANDREW: Music.

LINDA: I see. Not 'young people'?

> *Lights go to grey.* SIMON *makes a note.*

ANDREW: What are you writing?

> LINDA *waves her arms like Peter Garrett. Lights back on.*

LINDA: Every workplace needs a mediator. Do you intervene in this dispute?

ANDREW: I would be undermining Colin.

LINDA: So you'd back him all the way?

ANDREW: Is he right?

LINDA: He is your General Manager.

ANDREW: But is he *right*?

LINDA: Why?

ANDREW: May change my opinion.

SIMON: But you haven't got an opinion.

ANDREW: Yes, I have. / What are you writing?!

SIMON: Well, I haven't heard it yet.

ANDREW: That doesn't mean I don't have one.

SIMON: How can we judge you if you refuse to tell us what you're thinking?

ANDREW: 'Judge me'? Can I borrow your pen so I can write that down?

LINDA: You have been asked how you would handle a simple conflict resolution and we still haven't got an answer. That is not an opinion, that is my professional assessment. Okay? / Moving on.

ANDREW: Hold it.

LINDA: Are you raising your voice?

SIMON: [*to* LINDA] This is what they're talking about.

ANDREW: Who?

LINDA: We've taken some soundings.

ANDREW: I'm not a dolphin.

LINDA: Spoken to clients, colleagues. Casuals. The consistent response seems to be that you have difficulty keeping a level head in a crisis.

SIMON: Is that right?

ANDREW: No, I am very good under pressure.

SIMON: You're a bass player.

ANDREW: Yeah, and the lead singer is lying on the floor in the band room crying for no reason, the drummer is going through withdrawals halfway through the first set, cold sweat, shaking like a leaf. The business of music is crisis management.

*The tinnitus sound begins.*

LINDA: But what do you do in the real world?

ANDREW: Consult with the relevant parties and then make a decision.

SIMON: You make the decision?

LINDA: Because you're the boss?

ANDREW: Yes.

LINDA: And everybody back in the office? What about them? Who are they?

ANDREW: Colin, Jill and the casuals

LINDA: No, no. You misunderstand. *Who* are *they*?

ANDREW: The staff …? Is that what you mean?

LINDA: And the staff all work for you, do they?

*Lights go to grey.*

ANDREW: When did you get your HR degree?

SIMON: Irrelevant.

ANDREW: Disagree.

SIMON: Oh-ah.

ANDREW: Is this a school project or something?

SIMON: Answer the bloody question.

> LINDA *waves her arms like Peter Garrett. Lights back on.*

ANDREW: Nobody 'works' for me. Some people report to me and I am terribly sorry about that, but that's how the org chart is structured. Not my choice, that's just how it works.

SIMON: Because you're 'The Boss'?

ANDREW: I am the Director of Music. Co-CEO. And I report to the board. Right?

SIMON: What about Col? Is he 'The Boss' as well?

ANDREW: Colin is my Co-CEO.

SIMON: Titles.

ANDREW: What / was that? Simon?

LINDA: So, in your mind—Andy—

ANDREW: Andrew. / 'In your mind—'

LINDA: —is Colin 'The Boss' as well?

ANDREW: Yes. Colin is.

LINDA: Is that what you ask people to call you?

ANDREW: No.

LINDA: So, what do you ask people to call you? When you're relaxing with your … [*checking her notes*] … 'staff'?

ANDREW: Andrew. My name is Andrew.

SIMON: Not The Drewster?

ANDREW: Never.

LINDA: And what do they call Colin?

ANDREW: I don't know, the King of Patong?

LINDA: In your current Organisational Plan he is Co-CEO.

ANDREW: Currently, yes.

SIMON: Don't like the hierarchy, huh?

ANDREW: I'm fine with it.

SIMON: Doesn't sound like it. Sounds like you hate it. Resent it?

LINDA: Do you think we may have created a two-headed monster?

ANDREW: It's not in my remit to think about things like that.

SIMON: Remit.

ANDREW: You used to be on the 'grey list'.

LINDA: I read about this. Now. What is a 'grey list'?

ANDREW: A list of not-for-profits facing / defunding.

SIMON: Alright! Did we get the AusCo money or not?

*Silence.* LINDA*'s BlackBerry vibrates. She checks it.*

LINDA: Photocopier catastrophe. Michelle needs the code. Back in a second.

LINDA *exits. Lights go to grey. Silence.*

ANDREW: Simon, / this isn't a bloody 'catch-up', is it?

SIMON: You're sounding very fucking defensive for some reason—

ANDREW: Why the fuck are we meeting / *here*?

SIMON: It is easier for Linda.

ANDREW: She's working on your campaign?

SIMON: You don't know I'm going into politics.

ANDREW: What is she doing on the board?

SIMON: Good on her CV. Community Service. Valuable experience.

ANDREW: I'm not a fucking lab rat.

SIMON: No, you're a 'defensive, paranoid, isolated bully of a boss'.

ANDREW: Bullshit.

SIMON: Who told you I was standing for preselection?

ANDREW: Oh-ah. You have been betrayed.

SIMON: Did we get the money or not, smart arse?

ANDREW: No.

SIMON: Why not?

ANDREW: Too many targets. Not enough resources.

SIMON: But you're Lone Ranger-ing a fucking festival? /

ANDREW: What happened to Carmel?

SIMON: Are you trying to trigger me?

ANDREW: What the fuck happened to my predecessor?

SIMON: It is in the hands of the insurers and it is still playing out.

ANDREW: This is why we're meeting off-site—

SIMON: It's a schedule thing. This is / where Linda works.

ANDREW: She knows nothing about music. She knows nothing about young people. She hasn't even finished her degree.

SIMON *waves his arms like Peter Garrett. Lights back on.*

I did some googling on the break and guess what? She is studying HR part-time! Part-bloody-time? Are you fucking serious?

SIMON: WorkCover is a massive risk. If we don't cover our arses with policy, we could lose a helluva lot / more than a fucking …

ANDREW: Cover your arses? What are you gonna lose, Simon? What are you going to lose if your arse is left wide open?

SIMON: I refuse to lose my fucking house. My vineyard. I have a family. A reputation. We have indemnity. I am not / an idiot.

ANDREW: So what's on the line?—

SIMON: I am not giving up my future for you.

*The tinnitus peaks.* LINDA *enters with* JILL.

LINDA: Loud voices in the meeting room. Look who I found waiting in the corridor. Waiting like a little homeless person. This is Jill, isn't it …? Jill. How was Christmas, Jill? Did you get away?

SIMON: Jill went to Falls. Great Ocean Road.

LINDA: My brother's got a house at Moggs Creek. We hardly ever use it. Let me know next time you want to go down there, you can have the keys. I'm needed at the photocopier. Don't break anything.

LINDA *exits. Fluoro lights. Silence between the three. Then …*

ANDREW: / You don't have to be in here—

SIMON: What are you doing sulking around in the corridor?

ANDREW: It is fucking hot outside.

SIMON: Too hot to wait in the car?

ANDREW: It's forty degrees. The bush is burning!

SIMON: [*to* JILL] Go back to work.

ANDREW: We're delivering posters for the festival.

SIMON: [*to* ANDREW] *You* are?

ANDREW: Yes. We are.

SIMON: In a bushfire?

ANDREW: Somebody has to do it!

SIMON: Don't we have a marketing team for that?

JILL: You're looking at it.

SIMON: Fuck me swinging. I'm going to pay my rego.

SIMON *exits.* ANDREW *is alone with* JILL. *Pause.*

JILL: Road and Maritime Services?

ANDREW: Linda is our expert in Human Resources.

JILL: Linda couldn't find her cunt at a Christmas party.

ANDREW: See—that is—totally—inappropriate.

JILL: Are you recording this 'catch-up'?

ANDREW: You think I should?

JILL: Fuck, man. / Serious?

ANDREW: No. You think?

JILL: A hunting party. This is what happened to Carmel.

ANDREW: Forget about Carmel. / This has nothing to do with Carmel.

JILL: It's exactly the same! Listen. Linda called me over the holidays. Wanted to meet for a coffee. Talk about you. I didn't meet her.

ANDREW: Good.

JILL: We spoke on the phone.

ANDREW: What did you say?

JILL: It's confidential.

ANDREW: You are fucking / kidding—

JILL: Ando. That's what she told everybody.

ANDREW: She spoke to 'everybody'?

JILL: Colin, me. The casuals. The Advisory Group. You better make a recording of this, they are constructing your dismissal.

ANDREW: What the fuck am I gonna do?

*Lights go to grey.*

JILL: Fight. You have to fight.

*Beat.*

Simon gave me diamond earrings.

ANDREW: He gave you what?

JILL: Diamond studs for a Christmas present. He wants me to be grateful. This is how he … makes it sound like you're the most important girl in the world. 'We will fall apart with you' … and … This guy is a serial-sleaze-fucking-cunt. He always gets what he wants and he always gets away with it and somebody has to make him fucking pay!

*She jumps up. Lights back on. She takes a permanent marker and draws a large penis on the bare wall. Spurting out of the penis she writes: 'Simon is a cocksucker!'*

That cunt sucks fat wang.

ANDREW: Wang.

ANDREW *tries to scrub the graffiti off the wall.*

JILL: We have to fight this shit.

ANDREW: You just drew a fucking penis on the Road Traffic Authority. Permanent marker! Fuck. We are fucking fucked in the fuckshit. Get out of here!

JILL: No. / I want this confrontation! I want this fucker to see what I think!

ANDREW: You have to run! This is serious! No. You / don't—

JILL: I am not leaving!

ANDREW: Please!

JILL: Shut up.

SIMON *enters. Observes* ANDREW *trying to clean the board.*

*Pause.*

SIMON: Is that supposed to be my cock?

*Beat.*

An artist's impression of my ejaculate …? [*To* ANDREW] You drew this?

*Pause.*

Did you draw this cock and balls and sperm?

*Pause.*

JILL: No. / He didn't.

ANDREW: Yes. I did. / I take full responsibility! I drew the dick, okay?!

JILL: He's a liar! I drew it. I own it. How do you like it?

*Pause.*

SIMON: I was a aware that there was discussion about a new logo but … I don't think this is completely resolved. It's a little modest, don't you think?

JILL *pulls the earrings out of her pocket.*

JILL: You … make me … uncomfortable.

SIMON: You sound hysterical.

JILL: Give these to your wife.

*She slams the earrings onto the floor.*

*Pause.*

JILL *exits. Silence.*

SIMON: She comes from a family of liars. She is on a warning. I direct you to give her a written warning.

ANDREW *picks up the earring box.*

*Pause.*

She's been here too long. Put her on a warning.

*Beat.*

If you cannot manage your subordinates … you're cooked.

*Beat.*

Leadership demands action in a crisis.

*Pause.*

Colin was the first to express concerns about your poor behaviour.

ANDREW: He basically lives in fucken Thailand—

SIMON: You are a shit boss. You're history, / mate.

ANDREW: [*holding the earring box*] 'Give these to your wife' … What does that mean, do you reckon?

SIMON: She said no such / thing.

ANDREW: I am recording this meeting.

SIMON: Fuck off.

ANDREW: All my staff have Working With Children Checks. How about you?

SIMON: The board is non-operational.

*Beat.*

I have never seen that box before! Now, give it to me!

LINDA *enters.*

LINDA: Is Jill / okay?

SIMON: She's fine. Nothing to worry about. Get on with it. We have a process.

*Silence.* LINDA *sees the drawing. She sits.*

*Pause.*

LINDA: On a scale of one to ten—one being dismal and ten being exceptional—can you self-rate your capacity to manage a team?

*Pause.*

ANDREW: Eight point five?

LINDA *makes a note.*

LINDA: Quite high for a self-assessment.
ANDREW: Six.

LINDA *makes a note.*

LINDA: Okay. Thanks for coming in, Andrew.

*Silence.* LINDA *takes her phone and types out a text message, then …*

ANDREW: So what now?
LINDA: You leave and we have a discussion about you behind your back.
ANDREW: I'm sorry. I—hope we can … continue … See you at the festival.

*Pause.*

ANDREW *begins to exit.*

SIMON: Andrew …? Forget something?

*Beat.*

ANDREW: Oh, yeah. Thanks for meeting. Quite the custard fuck.

ANDREW *pockets the earrings. Exits. Silence.*

LINDA: You left them here alone?

*Pause.*

Why did you leave the room?
SIMON: You're serious.
LINDA: This is not my light-hearted face.
SIMON: I stepped out—*briefly*—to pay my car registration.
LINDA: You thought that was a good idea?
SIMON: The line was so short—
LINDA: Who drew this on my wall? Him or her?

*Beat.*

SIMON: It was him. He's appalling. He hates me like herpes.

LINDA: He thinks you're a 'cocksucker'.

SIMON: One man's opinion.

LINDA: You don't think it might have been the girl?

SIMON: Jill …? That suggestion is shocking to me … I'm hurt.

> *Pause.*

Right. Is there a conversation we need to have? Before I go to sub-committee?

LINDA: What did he put his pocket?

SIMON: No idea.

LINDA: Simon. What did he put in his pocket?

SIMON: Mints. He took my mints. Cunt.

> *Pause.*

What happens next?

LINDA: I write up recommendations for the board and we act.

SIMON: Send the draft to me.

> *Pause.*

I am asking you to keep me in the loop.

LINDA: Are you still directing me to sack this guy—?

SIMON: Yes.

LINDA: It doesn't stack up. He's doing a good job.

SIMON: Linda. Fiscally, he is a disaster. He is running a festival with no budget line, he is bullying his subordinates. Forcing programs on the membership and making financial commitments without checking for approval from the General Manager. He fucked up the AusCo. We miss out on the money. And that is why he was hired in the first place. He is a shower. And we have got him on toast. This is a clear case of reckless financial and emotional incompetence. Well done!

LINDA: You were right: small to medium is a nightmare.

SIMON: Yeah. But the young people make it all worthwhile.

> *He exits.* LINDA *approaches the graffiti. She tries to remove it.*

> *Lights go to grey.*

*SCENE TEN: SONG*

*This scene switches fluidly between the studio and the court action.*

ANDREW *sings. As the song goes on, we realise he is in the studio. At the end of the song,* JILL *appears. She has studio headphones around her neck.*

JILL: Neuman is so warm. So crisp.

ANDREW: Do you love it?

JILL: Thanks for the gear. It's a loan—and I won't forget it.

ANDREW: I know. Just …

JILL: What?

ANDREW: How did you do it?

> *Change to court action.*

PERKINS: The Act is appalling. It is almost impossible to prove psychological injury in the workplace. Justice is smoke in your hands. Today. It doesn't matter who said what to whom and why or when you were excluded or when you were bullied and you were—

LEANNE: There is no question. / We know that … Sorry. Yes.

PERKINS: But we must close our eyes to history. *Today* is all about *capacity*. From what date were you unable to work to what date you are capable to go back to work.

ANDREW: They injured me.

PERKINS: That is your *opinion*.

ANDREW: Have you read my medical reports?

PERKINS: Yes.

LEANNE: The reports are not strong.

PERKINS: *They* have two psychiatrists.

LEANNE: And we only have one psychologist and a GP.

PERKINS: The court is not impressed with psychologists. And GPs?

ANDREW: Not impressed?

PERKINS: Psychiatrists? Now you've got something.

ANDREW: Nobody ever said anything about that. Not even my doctor—

PERKINS: He recommended the psychologist?

ANDREW: Yes, *she* did. She knew a good one and she—she got me in.

PERKINS: But a psychologist cannot prescribe *medication*. Psychiatrists can prescribe medication and commit you to a treatment facility. Have you been hospitalised? Any time spent in a mental facility? At all? Because that could / really be— Yes. I understand … Yes.

ANDREW: They made me sick. I *am* sick. I fucking shake and I can't make decisions. Jesus. I play back every conversation, every detail, every choice. I am living that year on repeat. I hate every bone in my body.

PERKINS: Are you on medication right now?

ANDREW: Fuck yeah. Zoloft.

PERKINS: One hundred?

ANDREW: Absolutely.

PERKINS: Well. That's something.

ANDREW: Hey! I am so fucking sorry that I am not in a mental home—

PERKINS: Two psychiatrists win. That's all.

ANDREW: They are quacks! They were paid by the insurer and I fundamentally disagree with their reports. With the second quack especially. Mr *Finkle*, what a nut job. He started recording my session with a fucking Sony dictaphone—didn't ask my permission—I tell him to turn it off—he tells me I'm paranoid.

PERKINS *starts flipping through the folder.*

*Finkle* is a fucking liar.

PERKINS: Be specific.

ANDREW: He says. Okay. He says—I wasn't Co-CEO.

LEANNE: I saw that too. / What's that about? Why would he say that?

ANDREW: It's not true! / That is in the Strategic Plan, that's not just me.

PERKINS: He got that from the Chairman. 'Simon' somebody—is that right?

LEANNE: Simon said that on the record.

PERKINS: Simon doesn't like you at all, does he?

ANDREW: I want to burn that / fucker down. He actually believes that Brandis is a gift from God.

PERKINS: Let it go. Today is *capacity*. Nothing to do with retribution!

ANDREW: *Ambush meetings* what about them?

PERKINS: I know, I agree. Linda from HR …?

LEANNE: Appalling. Central casting psychopath. And Simon?

PERKINS: Idiot. Pure and simple.

ANDREW: Dunce cap in the corner.

PERKINS: Hear, hear.

ANDREW: Just got elected to / State Parliament.

PERKINS: Who would vote for that mountain goat?

ANDREW: They sold their own building.

PERKINS: Yes, I don't understand why?

ANDREW: Nine hundred thousand dollars.

PERKINS: Is that all? / For a heritage building in the CBD? How do you fuck that up? Good God.

ANDREW: I know. And. Now …? What the fuck are they doing? They run a Facebook page. Where did all the money go? He re-zoned the joint.

PERKINS: Of course.

ANDREW: It's going to be serviced apartments. Makes me sick to my stomach every time I / go past.

LEANNE: They constructed your dismissal, because you pissed off the wrong people.

*The tinnitus peaks.*

*Beat.*

PERKINS: Did you really play with Powderfinger?

ANDREW: Sat in for a tour.

*Beat.*

PERKINS: Guitar?

ANDREW: Bass.

PERKINS: Sing?

ANDREW: When I had to.

PERKINS: My brother sings because he wants to. He works with a few companies in Austria. Fluent—German. Wants to be a jazz singer. And the jazz singers want to sing opera. Can't have it both ways. But he has a beautiful voice. Really. When I was a teenager, I would record him on cassette and play it back in the car on road trips—sounded like a … I loved it. Miss it?

ANDREW: Like sunlight.

PERKINS: Been on any benefits? Any other work I should know about?

ANDREW: Some teaching. Trying to get back into production.

PERKINS: So you're demonstrating capacity to work.

*Beat.*

ANDREW: My marriage broke up. If that helps.

LEANNE *and* PERKINS *make notes.*

LEANNE: How long had you been married when she left?
ANDREW: How do you know she left?

*Beat.*

About a year.

LEANNE *and* PERKINS *make notes.*

PERKINS: This is fifty-fifty. The court likes *Finkle*. He is respected. But I've seen weaker cases win and I've seen stronger cases lose. So. What are you *instructing* me to do? Are you instructing me to go and ask them if they would like to make an *offer* of settlement?

*Beat.*

ANDREW: / Yes.
PERKINS: You want me to do / that?
ANDREW: Yes—
PERKINS: This is your *instruction*?
ANDREW: Yes! This is my instruction, Mr Perkins! / Why not?! Why not?!
PERKINS: Excellent! Excellent! And so we *begin*!

PERKINS *exits.* ANDREW *is alone with* LEANNE. *Silence.*

LEANNE: If you want a coffee—go and have a coffee. I have to— next— client—so I'm just—head down—spreadsheet up ... got some work.
ANDREW: How long is this going to take?
LEANNE: Two hours, two days. / Who knows?
ANDREW: Two days?
LEANNE: There's nothing you can do—except wait. The café at the train station is actually pretty good.
ANDREW: He's like a character in a play. Isn't he?
LEANNE: They all are. Larger than life. Have to be.
ANDREW: The woman with the black eye.
LEANNE: Yeah.
ANDREW: Her barrister looks like a young Nick Cave.

LEANNE: You think?

ANDREW: The gown.

LEANNE: He's a serious young talent.

ANDREW: Her case …

LEANNE: … is completely / different to yours.

ANDREW: Because you can see the evidence.

LEANNE: You can't compare.

ANDREW: I'm not—I'm just saying.

> *Pause.*

What's going to happen to her?

LEANNE: She has good representation. He's a fighter.

ANDREW: She's just a kid.

LEANNE: Yeah. I know. She's a semi-regular. That's right.

ANDREW: I don't have any money.

LEANNE: I know your situation.

ANDREW: I can't afford to pay you if we lose.

LEANNE: Andrew. It's not going to be like that.

ANDREW: Perkins said fifty-fifty.

LEANNE: He has a strategy / and you have trust him. He runs these cases every week.

ANDREW: I know. But after two years of fights and forms and interviews and anti-depressants and suicide. If I end up in debt after all of this / shit …

LEANNE: Hold it. Hold it. Did you …?

ANDREW: Did I what?

LEANNE: You attempted suicide. That's not in the paperwork.

> *Pause.*

It is a significant piece of evidence.

> *Beat.*

If we're going to win, we need the details. How did you do it? Andrew?

> *Pause.*

How were you planning to kill yourself?

ANDREW: This—this—doesn't matter.

LEANNE: We are constructing a persuasive argument to prove that damage was done. It's nothing to be ashamed of.

ANDREW: I'm not ashamed, / I'm just—
LEANNE: Okay. What are you? Andrew?

*Pause.*

A lot of people think about it. Lot of people. You'd be surprised. But … were you just thinking about it or were you actually going to do it? That's the difference. Did you have the idea, or did you really think about it? Did you have a strategy? Did you implement a / plan?
ANDREW: Might just stop you there.
LEANNE: Did your GP know about this?
ANDREW: / And—okay.
LEANNE: Did she implement a health management plan?
ANDREW: Yep.
LEANNE: Got you into the psychologist because of this?
ANDREW: Yes.
LEANNE: Okay.
ANDREW: I thought about it.

*Beat.*

LEANNE: How often?
ANDREW: Few times. But not since the counselling, not since the medication. / That has really—
LEANNE: Did you purchase any equipment?
ANDREW: Scch? Purchase 'equipment'.

*Pause.*

Yes. I did. Yeah, you got me.
LEANNE: Like what?
ANDREW: I didn't keep the receipts.
LEANNE: What exactly did you buy?
ANDREW: Roll of gaffer and a pipe.
LEANNE: Gaffer?
ANDREW: Tape.

LEANNE *starts typing notes into her laptop.*

It's a black tape—fabric base—strong. Industry standard.
LEANNE: What kind of pipe?
ANDREW: Flexible tubing. Like a vacuum cleaner.
LEANNE: So, 'hose', not 'pipe'.

ANDREW: I s'pose. Yeah. Got it at Bunnings. Available by the metre.

LEANNE: How many metres did you purchase?

ANDREW: I purchased five.

*He watches her type.*

You type fast … This is going into my notes.

LEANNE: Your case is an organic document. This is critical information.

ANDREW: I live in a small town. You know?

LEANNE: Yes, I know. I live here too. Cretins and bogans and— What was it?

ANDREW: I don't remember. Look. I don't know how much context I want to give them. I don't know if I am comfortable with Simon and Linda knowing just—what was going on in my—garage. You know what? I might just go an' get a coffee—

LEANNE: You said you can't drink coffee.

ANDREW: I am drinking metaphorically.

LEANNE: You're not going anywhere.

ANDREW: I need to clear my head—

LEANNE: I'm not letting you out of my sight. Not now. We're too close.

*Change to the studio.*

JILL *is showing a microphone to* ANDREW.

JILL: You can see the difference, can't you?

ANDREW: Certainly hear it.

JILL: All the little imperfections. I love it.

ANDREW: Permanent loan.

JILL: I can pay you in session time.

ANDREW: Great.

JILL: If you know it's here, you have to come down to play too, right?

ANDREW: Get me out of the house.

JILL: We can cut a demo for you—

ANDREW: Just … If you can use it. That's great.

JILL: A lot of songs in this.

ANDREW: You bet.

PERKINS: They're offering medical to date.

JILL: This is like a thousand dollars brand new—

*Change to the airlock.*

PERKINS: A thousand bucks.

JILL: It's a lot of money.

ANDREW: One thousand dollars?

PERKINS: That's just a guess—for the / consultations.

ANDREW: They already offered two and a half grand at the— / What's it called?

PERKINS: At the / conciliation?

ANDREW: The meeting—yes, with Peter Dymond—

PERKINS: Conciliation?

ANDREW: That's it.

PERKINS: They offered you two and a half?

ANDREW: / Yes. They offered me money. Back then.

PERKINS: Medical plus … two and a half …? / You see, I did not know that.

LEANNE: We didn't know that, Andrew.

*She types on the laptop.*

ANDREW: Peter didn't tell you?

LEANNE: How was the offer presented?

ANDREW: They called me—

LEANNE: A phone call?

PERKINS: Before the meeting? / They called you?

ANDREW: Yes. Before we'd even had the hearing—they called me.

PERKINS: Before the hearing?

ANDREW: Yes.

LEANNE: They offered you two and a half / thousand dollars? Before the hearing? Is that correct?

ANDREW: No—they—well—yes! Why am I saying 'No'? Yes! That's what they did. They called me and—somebody called me and it was Peter—he called me and said they were offering one thousand and—

PERKINS: That's unusual.

ANDREW: Is it?

LEANNE: They phoned before you went to / conciliation. One thousand dollars.

PERKINS: They started at one thousand flat?

ANDREW: Yes.

PERKINS: How did they get / to *two and a half*?

ANDREW: Peter called me and said they were offering a thousand bucks and I told them to forget it and they called back and offered two thousand and then on the day—on the day of the hearing they went up to two and half thousand and Peter told me—I should reject it—because if they were escalating so quickly, then—he thought their case was falling apart. So—

PERKINS: You rejected two and a half thousand dollars.

ANDREW: That's right.

PERKINS: Shit.

ANDREW: I should have said 'Yes'?

PERKINS: No. / That is not what we're saying.

LEANNE: Two and a half grand?

PERKINS: We are in a good position—

ANDREW: How is this a better position?

PERKINS: Is there anything else that I don't know?

LEANNE: Andrew?

ANDREW: No.

PERKINS: Are you sure?

ANDREW: What can you guarantee me?

PERKINS: Nothing.

ANDREW: Exactly. Exactly! And what if I only get half of that?

PERKINS: My mission is to get a deal that you feel is fair.

LEANNE: Mr Perkins?

ANDREW: No!

LEANNE: It's not in the notes / but …

ANDREW: Leanne, I said 'No'.

PERKINS: What is it?

ANDREW: Nothing.

PERKINS: Have you been working?

ANDREW: No.

PERKINS: Offer of employment?

ANDREW: Nothing like that.

LEANNE: Andrew attempted suicide.

*Beat.*

PERKINS: How?

*Change to the studio.*

JILL: Reverse engineering.

ANDREW: I love it.

JILL: I bought all the old PAR cans from Staccato, / all the amps and the gear.

ANDREW: Oh, you're kidding.

JILL: Fire sale prices. I packed a storage locker with all / this old Staccato shit and—

ANDREW: Oh, you didn't. Did you?

JILL: I met with Georgie and she was great. She was going to run this series of pieces on this new venue of mine and she asks me where it's going to be and I'm sitting in this meeting and I realise … I have got no idea what I am talking about.

ANDREW: You know how to run a venue.

JILL: But the last thing in the world that I want right now is run a venue—and so I say, 'I've just decided … it's going to be a festival'.

She looks me in the eye and says, 'There's already so many festivals out there, what's different about yours?'

And I talk about Second City and what we were planning to do before they shut us down and out of nowhere—I don't have any words—I start to sweat, and I start to shake and—she puts her hand on my wrist and says, 'Jilly, are you okay?' And that's it. I am history.

Wailing like an ice baby—so embarrassed. She's this big music businesswoman and I don't wanna look like fucking kid in front of her and I am crying in her office so bad that she—she shuts the door because of my bawling—this sobbing—tears deep from my belly. I don't think the howling will ever stop and she …

Two hours, two days later, I don't know … I stop. I am an idiot. Drowned in my own tears. Tapped out. And Georgie says, 'Is there anything I can do?'

You forget what it's like to hear stuff like that. Foreign language.

ANDREW: Georgie's the best—

JILL: Yes, she is. The bomb. My mentor.

*Beat.*

ANDREW: You got yourself a high-powered mentor.

JILL: Yeah. I got me one of them, yeah.

ANDREW: Fantastic. So … how does it work, do you meet for coffee?

JILL: Yeah—we meet for coffee, but we drink peppermint tea and go to yoga. I dream.

ANDREW: And then what?

JILL: The future. What does the future look like for me? You know? I force myself to map out a—chart of what the next five years might hold and … The future is fucking … scary. All I can do is see myself bashing away at a database and I don't know what to do and I start to panic because my future is a big black hole of stupid. I am terrified and I open my eyes and I am breathing like a marathon, heart is triple-time kick drum—lungs about to explode, I open my mouth and I can't hear the scream, and this is the answer to your question. Ando. This is the moment that I realise that without music in my life … I will die.

*Change to the airlock.*

PERKINS: Are you sure you were attempting to kill yourself?

ANDREW: Yes. I am / sure.

PERKINS: So, what were you going to do? Pills? Drugs? Hanging …? What …? What was your solution?

ANDREW: Started the engine. Went to sleep. Woke up with a migraine.

PERKINS: Classic. Should be in the notes. The GP at least. Fuck it. Okay. At least we know.

ANDREW: Yes, we all know now.

PERKINS: Nothing to be ashamed of. Do you want to accept the first shitty offer where you get nothing—or do you want to reject it? Instruct me!

ANDREW: Is that what / you're advising?

PERKINS: What are you instructing? / You have to instruct me!

ANDREW: Fuck. Yes. Reject it. Reject it!

PERKINS: Excellent. What do you want to counter?

ANDREW: What do you think we / should say? Okay.

PERKINS: Full medical and fifty-two weeks!

ANDREW: Sounds good.

PERKINS: They will reject it out of hand. Fifty-two weeks—it starts at ninety per cent! But are you comfortable with this counter?

ANDREW: Fuck yes. I *instruct* you! Make my *counter*!

PERKINS: I understand your *instruction*!

PERKINS *exits. Silence.*

ANDREW: I really think this is a huge mistake—

LEANNE: He has to know / everything.

ANDREW: Is he going to tell them I tried to top myself?

LEANNE: He is trying to get you some justice.

ANDREW: You told me to forget about justice.

LEANNE: That was just to calm you—the fuck—down! Jesus! You didn't come here prepared for a fight, you came for another briefing, we are running as fast as we fucking can. What more do you want?

ANDREW: I want them to admit liability.

LEANNE: But that's / just not going to happen—that is not what today is about.

ANDREW: They chew through staff like Tim Tams. They have to be held to account!

LEANNE: These plastic bags have forced that board to mount a defence. They have been meeting with insurance agents because of this, writing statements and finding witnesses, focusing on their policy vacuum. No matter what happens today, the board of Staccato will never forget you.

PERKINS *arrives back.*

PERKINS: They rejected the fifty-two weeks. They are offering thirty-five. Full medical. That's a number that suggests they do not want to go into court.

LEANNE: That's right.

PERKINS: Andrew. Do you want to go in there?

ANDREW: If we go in … what happens in the end?

PERKINS: You may walk out with nothing at all.

ANDREW: But they're offering thirty-five.

PERKINS: In *this* negotiation. Take your tax out and you've still got something. Okay. You can see the options. Now. Tell me. What is your instruction?

ANDREW: I want the madness to stop.

LEANNE: Good / decision.

PERKINS: I'll inform the defendants. Congratulations.

ANDREW: But … this isn't madness. This is my life.

*Beat.*

And I want to run it.

PERKINS: What about their offer?

ANDREW: I do not give a flying fuck about their shitty offer.

PERKINS: The money is on the table. I suggest you think about your health.

ANDREW: My life is worth more than thirty-five weeks and medical. I want to run my *case*. I want to go into court. This is my *instruction*!

PERKINS: I'll inform the defence. Here we go!

> PERKINS *exits. Long silence.*

LEANNE: Did you really draw a giant cock on the wall at the ambush meeting …? A permanent-marker penis? That 'wang'. Was it really you?

ANDREW: Nobody else in the room.

LEANNE: What about Jill? She was there.

ANDREW: How do you know?

LEANNE: She gave evidence.

ANDREW: For them?

LEANNE: No. She's on our side.

> *Pause.*

Who drew the wang?

ANDREW: It must have been Linda.

> *Change to the studio.*

JILL: And that's it. Decision made. Clear as a cowbell. I cannot test and tag my way to the top. I want to shape the silence. Work with little bits of genius. I go back to Georgie and I say, 'My future is in the studio. I wanna open a studio. Build my own label. Get my artists airplay and headline live shows. I want to be a producer.' There's this pause and she smiles and says, 'That's fantastic'. Felt like a grown-up. It makes sense—she helps me with the Business Plan. Walks me through the legal stuff. This is it. This is mine. It's not much—

ANDREW: It's a beginning. Your label. What are you going to call it?

JILL: Strategic Plan.

> *Beat.*

ANDREW: Really?

JILL: No, I just wanted to see your face when I said it.

ANDREW: Fuck me—

JILL: Your eyes were on stalks, like a cartoon. 'Really?'

ANDREW: What are you gonna call your label?

JILL: Deathtrap Records.

ANDREW: Oh—that's, that is gangster.

JILL: It's cool—

ANDREW: Scare the punters into buying the pressings.

JILL: 'DTR'. The logo is awesome.

ANDREW: I bet. I bet … The logo … Shit … Oh, man. It's good to see you.

JILL: Thanks for the gear.

ANDREW: It's fine, it's fine … it's all good.

JILL: So, what are you doing?

ANDREW: Promoting some new bands. I've got a couple of people I want you to consider. I think you'd be perfect for them and … Deathtrap Records is going to be successful, so I'm trying to associate with you as much as I possibly can.

JILL: Yeah, but what do you do for a real job?

ANDREW: I don't know yet. Got any ideas?

> *Pause.*

JILL: Did you really play bass in Powderfinger …? That's what they said in court … Is it true?

ANDREW: One tour. I sat in—John hurt / his hand and …

JILL: You learned the whole set list in two and half days.

ANDREW: Five days.

JILL: Powderfinger … I mean, they're pretty shit. But that's pretty cool. I may need some session players. You interested?

ANDREW: Maybe.

JILL: It's a high-pressure environment.

ANDREW: I'm in a good place.

JILL: Yeah. Me too.

> *Beat.*

ANDREW: Okay. I gotta go.

> *He doesn't move.*

JILL: You don't look like somebody who is trying to leave the music business.

ANDREW: I am. I'm going …

JILL: Where?

ANDREW: Home.

JILL: Wow. What are you doin' at home?

ANDREW: Repair some damaged gear.

JILL: What are you really doing?

*Pause.*

ANDREW: I go online, search up all the bands I used to listen to. Nick Cave, the Velvets, Watch them. Volume down and—The Church, The Stooges, The Pixies … fuck. Midnight Oil. Some of their early stuff is surprisingly good. But I always come back to my first loves …

JILL: / The Clash. The Pistols. The Jam.

ANDREW: The Pistols. The Clash. The Jam. Yeah … I'm going to spend this afternoon watching Paul Weller sing 'Going Underground' on repeat. I love that clip. Twenty-two forever—dressed to kill. Demanding justice. Smashing out the chorus and then the key change. I join him for the 'scream' and 'shout' … and end up pretending that I'm … I still have skin and it still tingles.

*Silence.*

JILL: Do me a favour.

ANDREW: What's up?

JILL: Stick around for a few hours.

ANDREW: Oh, I gotta go.

JILL: Yeah, you're so busy.

ANDREW: I don't want to trigger you or anything.

JILL: Shut up. Old man.

ANDREW: Old man?

JILL: Okay. I got a new prospect and I want your opinion. Listen to this.

*She puts buds in his ears—he smiles. Silence.*

ANDREW: You recorded this …? With Mr Neuman … That bass. You've got a gift, just—feels so prominent, but it's not in your face. It's great. Who are they?

JILL: Culture of Fear.

ANDREW: Serious? Oh-ah … Do I hear a B3 in there?

JILL: Do you like this sound …?

ANDREW: Yes. I do. Great job.

JILL: Thank you.

    *Pause.*

ANDREW: Yes. This is beautiful.

    *Silence. Lights snap out.*

*POST-SHOW MUSIC*

*Style Council: 'Walls Come Tumblin' Down'.*

## THE END

GRIFFIN THEATRE COMPANY PRESENTS

# A STRATEGIC PLAN
# BY ROSS MUELLER
# 27 JANUARY - 11 MARCH

**Director** Chris Mead
**Designer** Sophie Fletcher
**Lighting Designer** Verity Hampson
**Sound Designer and Composer** Steve Francis
**Design Assistant** Tyler Hawkins
**Stage Manager** Grace Nye-Butler
**With** Briallen Clarke, Matt Day, Justin Smith,
Emele Ugavule

**SBW STABLES THEATRE**
**27 JANUARY - 11 MARCH**

THEATRE COMPANY

Production Sponsor          Government Partners

nabprivate    nab          Australian Government    Australia Council for the Arts    NSW GOVERNMENT | Arts NSW

Griffin acknowledges the generosity of the Seaborn, Broughton & Walford Foundation
in allowing it the use of the SBW Stables Theatre rent free, less outgoings, since 1986.

## Executive Summary

*A Strategic Plan* is a comedy. It tackles pathological behaviour in the workplace and asks the question: what is the value of art? It is dedicated to Georgina Capper for her humour, her love and her strength.

## Overview

Nobody gets rich in the not-for-profit (NFP) arts sector. It is a passion industry, relying on professional artists bringing established professional networks and inexhaustible work ethics for the benefit of a fragile organisation. Employees are under-paid, overworked and often unappreciated. This is the current model.

## Core Business

Banks do not employ musicians as Directors. Law firms do not seek counsel from visual artists. But the not-for-profit arts sector regularly encourages white-collar wearers to contribute pro-bono to a panel, a committee or a Board to help with the delivery of arts and culture programs. These people involve themselves for a variety of personal and professional reasons.

## Specifics

- Pro-bono fundraising and legal services are essential for the salvation and required reporting of a small to medium sized arts enterprise.

- It can look good on your CV to be involved in a Board. It may advance your standing in the community and give an individual a sense of power and influence.

- A professional can bring a whole new skill set to a committee. The objectivity of the outsider can be perfect pitch for a NFP and fertilise the ambitions of the organisation.

- When non-arts advisors become overtly operational they can destroy the very enterprise they were trying to save.

## Environment

*A Strategic Plan* was written during my Masters at the Victorian College of the Arts in 2015. At the same time, George Brandis was dissecting our industry and putting jobs in jeopardy. Companies disappeared overnight. Uncertainty-led programming choices and the visceral division between major companies and independent artists became cavernous.

## Conclusion

In 2015 the signs at the bus stops said we were living in an 'Ideas Boom' but moving forward jobs and growth have gone backwards. Poverty cannot be the cost of excellence. Australia needs a new Strategic Plan.

## Footnotes

I want to thank Lee Lewis and all at Griffin. Anthony Blair and Harry Baxter. I also want to thank Dr. Raimondo Cortese, Jeremy Cohen, Richard Murphett, Dr Chris Mead, Olivia Satchell, Dom Mercer and the actors at VCA 2015 for their assistance in the development of *A Strategic Plan*.

---

### Schedule A

*"The decision handed down in Canberra on budget day in May 2015 astonished everyone with its audacity. Without a hint of warning, Brandis peremptorily moved $105 million of the Australia Council's funding out of the agency, using it to set up a ministerial slush fund. He gave this the grandiose title of the National Program for Excellence in the Arts. The Australia Council's chair, Rupert Myer, was called at about 5pm on budget day; just hours before Hockey was due to release the budget papers. The agency's CEO, Tony Grybowski, cut short a family holiday in Britain and rushed back to Sydney. The sector was gobsmacked. No one was consulted. No one was even told. Brandis simply announced it in a budget night media release. He was the minister, after all.*

*What allowed Brandis to do this? In a word: power."*

– Ben Eltham, 2016

---

**Ross Mueller**
Writer

# DIRECTOR'S NOTE

*With the lights out, it's less dangerous*
*Here we are now, entertain us*
*I feel stupid and contagious*
*Here we are now, entertain us*
Nirvana, 1991

I saw 12 plays this week. This is relatively unusual for me, maybe I see three or four plays a week; it is not at all unusual though that this might be possible in a major city. And of course my experience is just a microcosm of what is available to any of us most days of the week: plays, musicals, performances, concerts, galleries, choirs, sculpture classes, poetry readings, live music, more, more than we could ever see, attend, buy a ticket for beckons in most suburbs at almost all hours. Why is this so?

Legendary rock poet Patti Smith recently spoke to the brief 'why do I write?' She didn't know. She nevertheless spoke with candour, humour and charm to the 'how'; she writes because her world is dense with poets, novelists, photographers and musicians both alive and dead, all still restless, urgent, curious and dynamic. And that of course was ultimately her answer to the why: 'because we can't simply live'.

Some reputable theorists argue that we make art primarily in times of excess and surplus, when we have the time and the money. You may immediately refute that with examples of astonishing paintings, poems, novels or plays made at moments of intense suffering or stress. Evolutionary biologists contend that art making is central to the way our brains have developed, to our very being in the world.

This question of the 'why' was taken up in a recent comparison of the London Olympics' opening ceremony with Brexit. Both contained narratives about Britain: one of innovation, culture and inclusion; the other rage and bullish nationalism. These contrasting stories read, for writer Frank Cottrell Boyce, as a clarion call: art and culture, at their core, are fuelled by reckless generosity and artists needed to get busy.

This play by Ross Mueller is about an artist and about artists of the future, but also about management, and managers. Are they fundamentally antithetical? A crippling feeling of opposition has become acute recently because, since WW2, many Western governments supported the arts but, in attempting to ensure public accountability, required artists be managed, submit to assessment, attain key measurable, explain the 'why'. But how do we assess artists? How do we measure art? How do we justify to government that the spend was/is worthwhile? Are the myriad intrinsic benefits enough? Are instrumental benefits meaningful?

Yet still we make art, immerse ourselves in it, are hungry for it, exist because of it.

What I love about this play is that it is about that hunger, a conversation about fear, rage and befuddlement, delight, seduction, joy and ultimately, generosity. It is also funny. And live.

Sounds like a strategic plan to me.

**Chris Mead**
Director

## Ross Mueller

### Playwright

Ross Mueller is an Australian writer. Ross' theatre-writing credits include: for Griffin and Sydney Theatre Company: *Concussion*; for Australian Theatre for Young People: *A Town Named War Boy*; for Malthouse: *Construction Of The Human Heart, I Can't Even*; for Melbourne Theatre Company: *Cold Light Of Day, The Ghost Writer*; for Playbox Theatre: *The Final Days of Johnny Deere, No Man's Island, Screamsaver*; for Sydney Theatre Company: *ZEBRA!* He has written six plays for ABC Radio National and had two children's books published by Allen and Unwin. Ross has won the New York New Dramatists Playwright Exchange, the Wal Cherry Award for Play of the Year, and was the Australian playwright at the International Residency of the Royal Court Theatre in London in 2002. He has been a mentor for the National Studio, and is currently the Fresh INK tutor for ATYP in Victoria and a freelance columnist.

## Chris Mead

**Director**

Chris specialises in developing new writing. Chris' theatre credits include: for Griffin: *The Modern International Dead, Quack*, which won Best New Play, Sydney Theatre Critics' Awards and the WA Premier's Literary Award; for NIDA: *Rare Earth*; for Malthouse: *Walking into the Bigness*, which won Best Performance for VCE Theatre Studies. Chris is Literary Director of Melbourne Theatre Company. Previous positions have included: Curator of the Australian National Playwrights' Conference; Literary Manager of Belvoir; Festival Director, International Festival for Young Playwrights; inaugural Artistic Director of Playwriting Australia; and Literary Manager, and Wharf 2LOUD Producer, of Sydney Theatre Company. Chris has a PhD from Sydney University, is an inaugural Australia Council Dramaturgy Fellow, and was a judge for the Windham Campbell Award (Yale) and part of New Visions New Voices at Washington DC's Kennedy Center. His monograph on institutional racism and outreach strategies was published by Currency House.

## Sophie Fletcher

**Designer**

Sophie's theatre credits include, as Set and Costume Designer: for Griffin: *Caress/Ache, Emerald City, Gloria*; for Griffin and Bell Shakespeare: *The Literati*; for Belvoir: *This Heaven*; for Darlinghurst Theatre Company: *Broken*. As Design Assistant: for Belvoir: *Babyteeth, Every Breath, Peter Pan*; for Melbourne Theatre Company: *Miss Julie*; for Opera Australia: *The Marriage of Figaro, The Ring Cycle*; for Sydney Theatre Company: *Gross und Klein, The Maids, Waiting for Godot*. Her film credits include, as Costume Designer: for Whitefalk Films: *Florence Has Left the Building* and as Production and Costume Designer: for Whitefalk Films: *How to Get Clean, Measuring The Jump, Shadow Self* and *Trespass*.

## Verity Hampson

### Lighting Designer

Verity's theatre credits include, for Griffin: *The Turquoise Elephant, Angela's Kitchen, Beached, The Bleeding Tree, The Boys, The Bull, the Moon and the Coronet of Stars, The Floating World*; for Griffin and Bell Shakespeare: *The Literati*; for Bell Shakespeare: *A Midsummer Night's Dream*; for Belvoir: *The Drover's Wife, The Blind Giant is Dancing, Ivanov, Is This Thing On?, Small and Tired, Ruby's Wish*; for Sydney Theatre Company: *Hamlet: Prince of Skidmark, Little Mercy, Machinal*, for which she won the Sydney Theatre Award for Best Mainstage Lighting Design. Verity's television credits include: for ABC: *Live at the Basement, The Roast*. She is a NIDA graduate with over 10 years' experience as a lighting and projection designer. Verity was awarded the Mike Walsh Fellowship in 2012, which took her to Broadway to work with Tony Award-winning projection designers 59 Productions.

## Steve Francis

### Sound Designer and Composer

Steve's theatre credits include, for Griffin: *A Rabbit for Kim Jong-il, The Bull, the Moon and the Coronet of Stars, Between Two Waves, Speaking in Tongues, Strange Attractor, This Year's Ashes*; for Bell Shakespeare: *Hamlet, Henry V*; for Belvoir: *Angels in America, Babyteeth, Baghdad Wedding, Capricornia, Gulpilil, Keating!, Paul, Parramatta Girls, Ruben Guthrie*; for Melbourne Theatre Company: *The Weir, The Sublime*; for Sydney Theatre Company: *After Dinner, The Battle of Waterloo, Disgraced, The Hanging, The Long Way Home, Mojo, Rabbit, The Removalists, Sex with Strangers, Switzerland, Travelling North, Tusk Tusk*. Steve's dance credits include, for The Australian Ballet: *Totem*; for Bangarra Dance Theatre: *Boomerang, Belong, Bush, Corroboree, Lore, Skin, True Stories, Walkabout*. His compositions for film include, for ABC: *The Turning* and *Stories I Want To Tell You In Person*. Steve's awards include the 2003 and 2012 Helpmann Awards for Best Original Score, and the 2003 award for Best New Australian Work; he won a Sydney Theatre Award in 2011 and 2014.

## Tyler Hawkins

### Design Assistant

Tyler's theatre credits include, as Costume, Set and AV Designer: for NIDA: *#KillAllMen, The Olympians*. As Costume Assistant: for STC: *King Lear, A Midsummer Night's Dream*. As Costume Assistant and Wig Stylist: for Belvoir: *The Wizard of Oz*. Art Finishing: for Belvoir: *Mother Courage and Her Children*. Tyler's film credits include: as Costume Designer: *Brown Lips*; as Costume Assistant: *Eaglehawk, Saint Lo*; as Costume and Set Assistant: *Measuring the Jump*; as Production Designer: 'Pyramid' by Twin Caverns.

## Grace Nye-Butler

### Stage Manager

This is Grace's first production with Griffin. Grace's theatre credits include: for Bell Shakespeare (national tours): *Othello, Hamlet, and Henry V*; for Belvoir: *Stories I Want To Tell You In Person*; as Assistant Stage Manager: for Belvoir: *The Blind Giant is Dancing, The Wizard of Oz, Corranderrk, Elektra / Orestes* and *Medea*. Grace graduated from the Western Australian Academy of Performing Arts (WAAPA) with an Advanced Diploma of Stage Management. She has also worked for Black Swan State Theatre Company, Speigleworld, Pacific Opera, Sydney Festival and RockCorps.

## Briallen Clarke

### Linda / Leanne

Briallen's theatre credits include: as a performer: for Griffin: *Hollywood Ending*; for Darlinghurst Theatre Company: *All My Sons, The Lunch Hour, The Young Tycoons*; for Ensemble Theatre: *Clybourne Park*; for Melbourne Art Centre: *Dreamsong*; for Sydney Theatre Company: *Hay Fever*; for Old Fitzroy Theatre: *Pork Stiletto*; as Producer: for Australian Theatre for Young People: *Stop Kiss*. Her television credits include: as actor: Nine Network: *Doctor Doctor*; as writer and a performer: for ABC: *Freshblood*. Briallen graduated from the National Institute of Dramatic Art in 2010.

## Matt Day

### Simon / Perkins

*A Strategic Plan* is Matt's first production with Griffin. His theatre credits include: for Melbourne Theatre Company: *North by Northwest, Scarlett O'Hara at the Crimson Parrot*; for Sydney Theatre Company: *Fred, Six Degrees of Separation, The Wonderful World of Dissocia*. Matt's film credits include: Dance Academy: *The Comeback, Dating the Enemy, Doing Time for Patsy Cline, Kiss or Kill, Love and Other Catastrophies, My Year Without Sex, Muggers, Muriel's Wedding, Scoop, The Sugar Factory, Sweet Country, Touch*. His television credits include: *A Country Practice, And Starring Pancho Villa, The Beast, The Blitz: London's Longest Night, The Commander: The Devil You Know, Green-Eyed Monster, Hell Has Harbour Views, The Hound of the Baskervilles, The Informant, Life Isn't All Ha Ha Hee Hee, The Love of Lionel's Life, My Brother Jack, The Outlaw Michael Howe, Paper Giants: The Birth of Cleo, Rake, Shackleton, The Snowy River: The McGregor Saga, Tangle* and *Underbelly: The Golden Mile*.

## Justin Smith

### Andrew

Justin's theatre credits include: for Griffin: *Clark in Sarajevo, The Floating World, The New Electric Ballroom*; for Bell Shakespeare: *Just Macbeth, The Servant of Two Masters, R and J, The Winter's Tale*; for Belvoir: *Cat on a Hot Tin Roof, The Threepenny Opera, Svetlana in Slingbacks*; for Sydney Theatre Company: *A Flea in Her Ear, Arcadia, The Cherry Orchard, Ruby Moon, The Wonderful World of Dissocia*. Justin's musical theatre credits include: *Billy Elliot: The Musical, Jesus Christ Superstar, Rent, Tick Tick Boom*. His television credits include: *Backberner, Bastard Boys, Deadline Gallipoli, Devil's Playground, Howzat! Kerry Packer's War, My Place, Queen Kat Carmel and St Jude, Secret City, Spirited, Stingers, The Straits, Tricky Business, Underbelly: Badness, White Collar Blue*. Justin's film credits include: *Angst, Around the Block, Being Venice, Burning Man, The Eye of the Storm, Sleeping Beauty*. In 2017 he will appear in *Pirates of The Caribbean: Dead Men Tell No Tales*.

## Emele Ugavule

### Jill

*A Strategic Plan* is Emele's first production with Griffin. Emele's theatre credits include: for Belvoir: *Twelfth Night, Mother Courage and Her Children*; for NIDA: *In the Blood, The Light in the Piazza, Woyzeck, Kasimir & Karoline, Sunday in the Park with George*; for Parade Theatre: *The Olympians*. Her television acting credits include: for ABC and Playmaker Media: *The Code*. She produced the AV series, *The Places We Call Home*, for Pacific Islanders in Communications, Cowbird & PBS, and has co-produced and directed independent music videos. Emele will perform as part of her collective Black Birds in the Joan's 2017 season. She is a 2014 graduate of the National Institute of Dramatic Art.

# ABOUT GRIFFIN

*"If you've ever sat in the theatre and thought, 'those actors are just too damn far away', then Griffin is for you."* – Concrete Playground

Located in the heart of Kings Cross – in the historic SBW Stables Theatre – Griffin has been dedicated to bringing the best Australian stories to the stage for the better part of four decades.

We're passionate about theatre that's written by Australians, about Australians, for Australians to enjoy. Iconic plays such as *The Boys, Holding the Man* and *The Heartbreak Kid* all had their world premieres at Griffin. And many of our nation's most celebrated artists started their professional careers with us – Cate Blanchett, David Wenham, Michael Gow and Louis Nowra to name a few.

Homegrown inspiration. By you, for you.

GRIFFIN THEATRE COMPANY
13 CRAIGEND ST
KINGS CROSS NSW 2011

02 9332 1052
INFO@GRIFFINTHEATRE.COM.AU
GRIFFINTHEATRE.COM.AU

SBW STABLES THEATRE
10 NIMROD ST
KINGS CROSS NSW 2011

BOOKINGS
GRIFFINTHEATRE.COM.AU
02 9361 3817

GTC
RHO
IEM
FAP
FTA
IRN
NEY

Australian Government

Australia Council for the Arts

NSW GOVERNMENT | Arts NSW

# STAFF

**Artistic Director & CEO**
Lee Lewis

**General Manager**
Karen Rodgers

**Associate Producer -
Development**
Will Harvey

**Associate Producer -
Marketing**
Estelle Conley

**Publicist**
Dino Dimitriadis

**Communications Associate**
Aurora Scott

**Program & Administration
Coordinator**
Lane Pitcher

**Strategic Insights
Consultant**
Peter O'Connell

**Production Manager**
Kirby Brierty

**Financial Consultant**
Tracey Whitby

**Finance Manager**
Kylie Richards

**Customer Relations Manager**
Elliott Wilshier

**Front of House Manager**
Damien Storer

**Front of House**
Maria Dimopulos, Alex
Herlihy, Renee Heys, Julian
Larnach, Jade da Silva,
Linda Popic

**Studio Artist**
Phil Spencer

**Web Developer**
Holly

**Digital Consultant**
Adrian Wiggins

**Brand and Graphic Design**
Re

**Cover Photography**
Brett Boardman

# OUR DONORS

Income from Griffin activities covers less than 40% of our operating costs – leaving an ever increasing gap for us to fill through government funding, sponsorship and the generosity of our individual supporters. Your support helps us bridge the gap and keep ticket prices affordable and our work at its best. To make a donation and a difference, contact Griffin on 9332 1052 or donate online at griffintheatre.com.au

## OUR DONORS

### Studio Program
Gil Appleton
James Emmett & Peter Wilson
Limb Family Foundation
Peter Graves
Ken & Lilian Horler
Sophie McCarthy & Antony Green
Rhonda McIver
Geoff & Wendy Simpson
Danielle Smith

## PRODUCTION DONORS

### THE HOMOSEXUALS OR 'FAGGOTS' 2017

### Presenting Partner
Rebel Penfold-Russell

### Production Patrons
Anonymous
Andrew Bell & Joanna Bird
Robert Dick & Erin Shiel
Richard McHugh & Kate Morgan
Bruce Meagher & Greg Waters
Richard Weinstein & Richard Bennett

### Production Partners
Gil Appleton
Tony Jones
Rodney Cambridge
Michael Hobbs
Steve Riethoff
Diana Simmonds

### LADIES DAY  2016

### Production Patrons
Robert Dick & Erin Shiel
Reay McGuinness
Richard McHugh & Kate Morgan

Bruce Meagher & Greg Waters
Richard Weinstein & Richard Benedict

### Production Partners
Cambridge Events
Michael Hobbs
Steve Riethoff
Annabel Ritchie
Diana Simmonds
Jenny & Peter Solomon

## SEASON DONORS

### Commission $12,500+
Darin Cooper Foundation
Anthony & Suzanne Maple-Brown

### Main Stage Donor $5,000 - $10,000
Peter Graves
Helen & Abraham James
Jon King
Don & Leslie Parsonage
Lee Lewis & Brett Boardman
Sue Procter
The Robertson Family Foundation
Merilyn Sleigh & Raoul de Ferranti

### Final Draft $2,000-$4,999
Gae Anderson
Stewart Baxter
Alex Byrne & Sue Hearn
Richard Cottrell
Mark Coulter
Bryony & Tim Cox
Tina & Maurice Green
Libby Higgin
Sophie McCarthy & Antony Green
Bruce Meagher & Greg Waters
David Nguyen
Peter & Dianne O'Connell

Pip Rath & Wayne Lonergan
Anthony Paull
Chris Reed
Westpac
Adrian Wiggins & Siobhan Toohill
Carole & David Yuile

### Workshop Donor $1,000-$1,999
Anonymous (3)
Ange Cecco & Melanie Bienemann
Antoinette Albert
Melissa Ball
Baly Douglass Foundation
Karen Bedford
Jane Bridge
Corinne Campbell & Bryan Everts
Terence Clarke
Russ & Rae Cottle
Michael Diamond
Tim Duggan
Ros & Paul Epsie
John & Libby Fairfax
Jennifer Giles
Judge Joe Harman
James Hartwright & Kerrin D'Arcy
John Head
Angela Herscovitch
Michael Hobbs
Peter Ingle
Margaret Johnston
Jennifer Ledgar & Bob Lim
Kiong Lee & Richard Funston
Richard & Elizabeth Longes
Elaine & Bill McLaughlin
Ruth Melville
Dr Wendy Michaels
Stephen Mills
Tommy Murphy
Jo Nolan
Patricia Novikoff
Ian Phipps
Martin Portus
Crispin Rice

Rebecca Rocheford Davies
Natalie Shea
Will Sheehan
Amanda and Michael Solomon
Ross Steele
Augusta Supple
Victoria Taylor
Stuart Thomas
Mike Thompson
Gayle Tollifson
Anna Volska
Judy & Sam Weiss
Paul & Jennifer Winch
Penny Young & Ian Neuss

**Reading Donor**
**$500-$999**
Anonymous (4)
Les Andersen
Wendy Ashton
Robyn Ayres
Michael Barnes
Penny Beran
Edwina Birch
Michael & Colleen

Chesterman
Terrence Clarke
Bernard Coles
Sally Crawford
Fiona Dewar
Louise Diamond
Max Dingle
Vicki Ditcham
Wendy Elder
Erica Gray
Sheba Greenberg
Anthony Gregg
Janet Grant
Jennifer Hagan
Stephanie & Andrew
Harrison
Jacqueline Hayes
Tim & Virginia Herlihy
Mark Hopkinson
Sylvia Hrovatin
Susan Hyde
Maria and Ross Kelly
C John Keightley
Ian & Elizabeth MacDonald
Carina Martin

Christopher McCabe
John McCallum
Stuart McLean
Dr Steve McNamara
Neville Mitchell
Catriona Morgan-Hunn
Steve & Belinda Rankine
Alex Oonagh Redmond
Roslyn Renwick
Annabel Ritchie
Karen Rodgers & Bill
Harris
Julianne Schultz
Nicola Scott
Diana Simmonds
Jann Skinner
Eric Dole & Mary Stollery
Catherine Sullivan &
Alexandra Bowen
Sue Thomson
Jennifer Watson
Simone Whetton

# OUR DONORS

**First Draft Donor**
**$200-$499**
Anonymous (5)
Priscilla Adey
Gregory Allen
Richard Archer
William Armitage
Anna Barker
Nikki Barrett
Pamela Bennett
Peter Best
Bodey Boland
Julie Bridge
Rob Brookman & Verity
Laughton
Wendy Buswell
Amanda Clark
Sue Clark
Silvia Colloca
Bryan Cutler
Susan Donnelly
Sarah Dunn
Claire Evans
Elizabeth Evatt
Robyn Fortescue
Brenda Gottsche
Janet Grant
Elizabeth Hanley
Will Harvey & Ester
Harding
David Hawke
Belinda Hazelton
Janet Heffernan
Karen Henoch-Ryugo
Danielle Hoareau
Mary Holt
Fiona Hulton
Suzanne Ingelbrecht
Diana Jefferson
Leslie Jesudason
Val Jory
Susan Kath
Gretel Killeen
David & Adrienne Kitching
Kaye Fairall Lee
Peta Leemen
Carolyn Lowry
Anni Macdougall
Rob Macfarlan & Nicole
Abadee

Stephen Manning
Prudence Manrique
Robert Marks
Louise McDonald
Duncan McKay
Keith Miller
Sarah Miller
Kate Mulvany
Margaret Murphy
Gennie Nevinson
Kerry O'Kane
Annie Page & Colin
Fletcher
Christopher Powell
Virginia Pursell
Gavin Roach
Bill Roberts
Tracey Robson
Ann Rocca
Ellen & Trevor Rodgers
Catherine Rothery
Gemma Rygate
Dimity Scales
Nicola Scott
Julia Selby
Roger Sewell
Elizabeth Shaw
Leigh Small
Rob Spence
Geoffrey Starr
Leslie Stern
Augusta Supple & Daniel
Rhodes
Barbara Tapsell
Mark & Susan Tennant
Simon Tolhurst
Lesley Turnbull
Benson Waghorn
Aviva Ziegler

We would also like to
thank Peter O'Connell for
his expertise, guidance
and time.

Current as of
28 November 2016

# GRIFFIN SPONSORS

Griffin would like to thank the following:

## Government Supporters

Australian Government | Australia Council for the Arts

NSW Government | Arts NSW

CREATIVE CITY SYDNEY

## Patron

S&W Foundation

## 2017 Season Sponsor

Re|

## Production Partner

GIRGENSOHN FOUNDATION

## Production Sponsors

nabprivate | nab

FOXTEL arts

## Foundations and Trusts

MALCOLM ROBERTSON FOUNDATION

COPYRIGHT AGENCY CULTURAL FUND

ROBERTSON FOUNDATION

GIRGENSOHN FOUNDATION

## Company Lawyers

MAR/QUE

## Associate Sponsor

Brett Boardman Photography

## Company Sponsors

TimeOut

THE UNIVERSITY OF SYDNEY PERFORMANCE STUDIES

Tatler SYDNEY

bourke street bakery

Rosenfeld, Kant &Co. Business & Financial Solutions

MOPPITY

CURRENCY PRESS

Coopers

FOUR PILLARS SMALL AUSTRALIAN DISTILLERY

169 DARLINGHURST

Qbt CONSULTING

SATURDAY PAPER

DESIGNKINGCOMPANY

Griffin Theatre Company is assisted by the Australian Government through the Australia Council, its arts funding and advisory body; and the NSW Government through Arts NSW.